THE STORY OF

P!NK

SPLIT PERSONALITY

THE STORY OF P!NK

SPLIT PERSONALITY

Paul Lester

OMNIBUS PRESS

London / New York / Paris / Sydney / Copenhagen / Berlin / Madrid / Tokyo

Cover designed by Fresh Lemon
Picture research by Jacqui Black

ISBN: 978.1.78038.986.8
Order No: OP55209

Exclusive Distributors
Music Sales Limited,
14/15 Berners Street,
London, W1T 3LJ.

Music Sales Corporation,
180 Madison Avenue, 24th Floor,
New York, NY 10016, USA.

Macmillan Distribution Services,
56 Parkwest Drive
Derrimut, Vic 3030,
Australia.

Every effort has been made to trace the copyright holders of the photographs in this book but one or two were unreachable. We would be grateful if the photographers concerned would contact us.

Typeset by Phoenix Photosetting, Chatham, Kent
Printed in the EU

A catalogue record for this book is available from the British Library.

Visit Omnibus Press on the web at www.omnibuspress.com

Contents

Contents

Introduction

Pink has never been very, well, pink – there's nothing particularly sugary or girly about this singer, songwriter and performer who has been part of our pop lives this century-so-far.

As a name, "Pink" is a red herring – and as a result it has been easy to misjudge her, to dismiss her as just another fluffy candy pop starlet when really she has more in common with her all-time heroine, Janis Joplin, than any number of here-today-gone-tomorrow girls in pretty dresses. A motorbike-riding, rifle-toting, tattooed, big-voiced belter and exponent of rocky pop and poppy punk who almost overdosed after experimenting with every Class A compound known to chemists, aged 16? I was going to say that, in terms of rock'n'roll credentials, Pink makes Janis look like Britney, but Ms Spears is hardly the epitome of the clean-living popstrel herself these days. She makes Janis look like Beyoncé? Yes, that works, for now, anyway – see: Houston, Whitney...

In a way, Pink raised the bar – or lowered it, depending on your view – for badly behaved ex-teen-pop queens this decade. Listening closely to all her albums for this book, it occurred to me that Pink has been Pink – that is to say, not-pink – since the word go. Most accounts have it that she started off as the R&B puppet of powerfully manipulative dance-pop svengalis before taking control of her career and becoming the all-snarling punky brat we know and love today, but even a cursory glance at the song titles on her 2000 debut album, *Can't Take Me Home*, suggest the change of direction on second release *M!ssundaztood* (2001) wasn't quite as dramatic as it seemed: 'Split Personality', 'Hell Wit Ya', 'Save My Life', 'You Make Me Sick', 'Let Me Let You Know' – standard pop lyric tropes if you like, or alternatively, early signs of the troubled but hugely successful recording artist who has in a way built an audience around the fact that she has never quite recovered from her messed-up childhood and wild-living adolescence.

If "troubled" and "successful" are Pink watchwords, there's a third: honest. She has never been less than forthright about her past and her problems, expressing – exposing – herself with gynaecological candour, and that has both shed light on her work and helped make her an unusually interesting character to observe these past 10 years. Pop may be sewn up these days by PRs who rarely let their charges reveal much about themselves to journalists in the hour or so that the latter are usually granted in a sterile hotel suite, but Pink is one of the few pop stars who cannot be contained, who shouts her mouth off and says the unsayable, often when her record company minions are least expecting it.

She talks in superlatives and extremes, as though every step she takes is emotionally draining and painful. Loyal, as she puts it, "to a fucking T", leaving the girl-group that kickstarted her career to go solo was not just "really tough" and "the hardest decision of my career" but in fact "the worst position I've ever been put in, in my life."

You get a sense of the mixed-up girl, who began writing

songs when she was 14, even in the early days of her career. The self-styled "chameleon" who would dye her hair green and walk out of rooms backwards to get attention seemed to be singing gospel in the church choir one minute, then being the "token white girl" in an R&B troupe the next. Either that or she'd be variously dancing in Philadelphia clubs, doing backing vocals for a hip-hop outfit called School Of Thought or yelling and thrashing about in local punk bands.

Sex is rarely off the agenda when you're talking to Pink. Then again, if you write a song like 'Fingers', about masturbation, you're probably going to be probed, if you'll forgive the disgusting imagery, a little about your private habits. On the record conversations about everything from her lesbian tendencies to the size of her husband's schlong are typical with Pink.

As for drugs, she's not exactly reticent about discussing her antics there, either. "Holy shit!" she once groaned, recalling her first visit to Amsterdam to a journalist. "I was 19 years old, I went straight from the airport to the Bulldog café, bought a thousand bags of weed and smoked them all by myself and then went on stage. It was a TV show and I was borderline collapsing on camera. The producer came on stage and said, 'Would you like to do that again, because that's the most awful performance I've ever seen in my entire career.' I looked at her and said, 'Do what?' It was halfway through dinner after the show when I came out of my coma."

She's no slouch in the self-examination department, either: no one does exorcisms-of-anguish like Pink, both in interviews and in songs. If she has built a career around her childhood pain, she is quick to acknowledge that she is not the only one who has suffered. "I've seen my dad cry four times in my life and one of them was when I played him [my song] 'Family

Portrait'. My mom cried for days and then it became this big thing: 'I didn't know you were so affected – let's talk.' I'm like, 'It was just a song. I'm fine!'"

Mostly, Pink does brash. Whether it's declaring, "I'm not Madonna's bitch" after refusing to kiss the queen of pop at the MTV awards, issuing feminist proclamations in gay bible *Attitude* or parrying accusations of hypocrisy after affirming the empowering nature of stripping off in public (in videos or photo sessions) for the sake of her art, Pink is never less than entertaining – and as the great woman herself has said, "Entertainment sometimes for entertainment's sake is ok." Hopefully in this book you will be entertained by Pink, and get some sense of her value not just as an entertainer, but as a complex, multifaceted, often confused human being whose real-life issues often spill over into her music, and whose music holds up a mirror to the wondrous mess that is her life.

Paul Lester, June 2009

Chapter 1

Family Portrait

"It's funny to me. People are documenting what I'm doing now and they think I'm some rabid, crazy, lunatic... whatever, and I'm so tame compared to how I used to be."

Pink wasn't always Pink, or for that matter P!nk, the precocious, electrifying R&B diva turned provocative, sexually aggressive, globally famous shock-pop-rocker with attitude, sing-shouting with infectious indignation about stupid girls, George Bush's inglorious war efforts and masturbation, whose mouth is caught in the world's media in a permanent semi-smile or scream, snarl or scowl.

The multimillion-selling, two-time Grammy-winning singer-songwriter (and sometime actress) was born Alecia Beth Moore in Doylestown, Pennsylvania, on September 8, 1979, although she got her nickname at an early age, even if accounts vary as to its derivation: it has been suggested that it came about as a result of a lurid incident when she exposed

1

herself at a summer camp when she was a child, causing her to blush pink with embarrassment; the singer has also intimated that it comes from her love of the Quentin Tarantino film *Reservoir Dogs* and her favourite character, Mr Pink, or simply from the colour she chose to dye her hair from the age of 10. Whichever is true, it stuck, and hardly anyone uses her birth name these days – in fact, when strangers attempt to do so, she recoils, almost as though she doesn't want to be reminded of the girl she once was.

The Moore family – Pink, her mother, Judy Moore (née Kugel), her father James Moore Jr and her older brother Jason – moved to Doylestown, a working-class suburb some 35 miles north of Philadelphia with a population of under 10,000, early on in her life. There, she attended Kutz Elementary School, Lenape Middle School, and Central Bucks West High School. Pink always stood out. From an early age, she recalls, the tomboy into Guns N' Roses would "dye my hair green and walk into a room with my clothes on backwards just to get a rise out of people." She has described hers as "the normal, average, fucked-up dysfunctional family" and alluded to her upbringing in that excoriating slice of arguably factual musical autobiography, the notorious 2002 hit single 'Family Portrait', where her mother was always crying and her father was always yelling and it was like "growing up in World War 3". Her parents fought bitterly and relentlessly. Though her childhood chronicled on her 2001 album, *M!ssundaztood*, seems to have been terminally miserable, she does have some happy memories of growing up around Philadelphia: "Camping. Running through the woods with my brother. There was a pit, a huge 30ft dirt ramp. We'd slide down it and kill ourselves. It was so much fun."

Besides, over the years the musician of mixed parentage –

her ancestors were immigrants from Ireland, Germany and Lithuania – has become reconciled with her past and has good things to say about her Jewish mum, an ER nurse, and Catholic dad, a Vietnam veteran turned boss of an insurance company. Mostly, anyway...

"I was angry for many years," she told a reporter in 2006. Today, she and her mother are "inseparable", but back then she "couldn't handle me. We get along fine now, but at the time it was tough. A lot of my rage in my songs comes from the unhappiness I felt as a child."

There is no denying the devastating impact that her parents' divorce, which happened when she was nine years old, had on the shy, sensitive, vulnerable pre-teen. That, as she remembers it, is when her out-of-control period began.

"My relationship with my parents now is as good as it has ever been," she admits, granting that "everyone is psychologically abused by their parents – isn't that what parents are supposed to do? [But] I didn't want my dad to leave [home] and I fought with Mum.

"[It began] when I was nine," she confirms the commencement of her wayward adolescence. "I started early but I'm glad because now I'm mellow."

There was nothing mellow about her teenage years, a period that saw her living with whichever friend would take her in and watching her friends drink and drug their lives away. One night Pink even had a gun pulled on her, although she apparently defused the situation by telling her assailant that he suffered from halitosis.

After her parents separated Pink moved in first with her mother, and then her father; for a period, she divided her time between the two homes. Her mother struggled to manage her increasingly unruly daughter. Reports vary as to what began

3

when – some have it that she began smoking cigarettes at nine and marijuana at 10-and-a-half – but what's certain is that, aged 12, Pink fell in with the local "bad guys" and soon after started skipping school, adorning her body with tattoos and piercings, and experimenting with hard drugs.

When she was 14, the burgeoning teen rebel, who sincerely believed children as young as 11 should be allowed to experiment freely with ecstasy, was taken by her mum to see a therapist, who she would tell "all kinds of crazy shit. Like, 'What did you do today?' Oh, I pictured breaking a bottle in half and slicing my teacher's throat with it."

In her mid-teens, Pink, the self-styled "walking conflict", was a strange mixture of off-the-rails immaturity and perverse precocity; she even visited her local library to research just how many illicit intoxicants she could consume without killing herself.

Unfortunately, this attempt at reason and cold logic didn't prevent her from almost self-destructing when she was 16. On Thanksgiving in 1995, two years after the death from an overdose of actor River Phoenix outside the Viper Room in Hollywood, Pink OD'd herself inside a Philadelphia nightclub. She had apparently already been drinking beer and smoking marijuana, and taking hits of, variously, crystal meth, ketamine, angel dust, ecstasy, cocaine and nitrous oxide aka laughing gas. Then she started dropping acid; lots of it. Suddenly, her lips turned blue and she lay down on the floor, expecting it to be her last night on Earth.

The trouble was, she was surrounded by users and abusers: all her friends were, as she puts it, "fucked-up, too", so for Pink this was normal behaviour for kids of her age. Even the deaths of several acquaintances from sustained drug abuse didn't dissuade her from taking them herself.

"My life was insane," she told journalist Caroline Graham in 2006, "but I knew nothing about mortality – until I buried three friends from heroin overdoses... I saw friends of mine die of drugs. You'd think that standing in a churchyard watching your friend being lowered into the ground would put you off doing drugs, but it never did."

However, the events of that fateful night in November 1995 did finally hit home, and, lucky to have survived, she vowed thereafter to give up drugs and go "clean": "I didn't go to rehab or Narcotics Anonymous," she said, "I just stopped, because being a singer really mattered to me and it was important to be in control."

Not that she stopped her wild ways altogether; far from it. She acknowledges that she was a bit of a handful, telling journalist Louise Gannon, "I was every mother's nightmare child. I was angry, I was confused, I was wild, I was trouble, I got expelled, I got arrested so many times my mum knew all the of the police by name in Philadelphia. Part of it was because I felt I didn't really fit in anywhere but part of it was because I was a natural-born rebel. I would do anything and I didn't care, and a lot of it was good fun."

Not for her mother it wasn't; indeed, realising that she could no longer cope with her anymore, she sent Pink to live with her father.

Jim Moore was a politically engaged veteran of the Vietnam War; his wife, Pink's step-mum, was also a nurse, who tended soldiers during the conflict. After years of denial and silence on the subject of the horrors that he'd experienced, when he turned 40 Moore decided he needed therapy himself, to exorcise the demons he'd been battling with since returning from the war. So he founded a group called the Vietnam Veterans Chapter 210 of Bucks County, its aim to hold fundraising events and provide succour, in the form of group sessions, for all of the county's veterans. Before Pink entered double figures she would go along to these meetings, where she would look on amazed as grown men broke down and wept, or she would join her dad as he helped dish out food at soup kitchens or went on marches for veterans' rights. Instead of being bored or even appalled, the young Pink was enthralled by all this activity. "I loved it," she said. "It was the fire under my feet."

Her dad was a larger-than-life character who Pink has described variously as "a bad-ass", "intense" and "insane". She has spoken in awed terms of her gun-toting, motorbike-riding dad, of his knowledge and experience of full-contact karate and guerrilla warfare and the fact that, for whatever reasons, he kept a stock of rocket-launchers in his garage.

While her mother was probably insufficiently strict, her father, a serious, authoritarian figure, went to the opposite extreme as a way of dealing with his hellishly intractable daughter. The pair would argue furiously. Nevertheless, Pink never had anything but the utmost respect for him. "I never believed in authority, I knew what I wanted to do, and I didn't like rules," she told the *Guardian* in 2006. "[But] I respected my dad because he would put me through a wall if I didn't. He was consistent, and I respected that. If he wanted to warn me, he'd count to three, but I only ever let him get to two-and-three-quarters. You don't fuck with Jim Moore – you just don't.

"He could kick your ass, he could make you laugh, or he could teach you something. He was a cool guy," she added.

Retaining that sense of childlike wonder, even worship, she calls him her "first rock star" (they would later perform a song together, 'I Have Seen The Rain', on her 2006 album, *I'm Not Dead*). Indeed, it was Jim Moore who first inspired Pink – who realised early on that she had a powerful singing voice, despite suffering from asthma throughout her childhood – to want to become a performer after he played guitar and sang songs to her from an early age.

She explains that his fiery temperament and eccentric demeanour were not the result of his foray in Vietnam; rather, fighting in the Far East, for which he volunteered, was a way of escaping his own troubled background – she claims that he was abused as a child – and miserable experience at Catholic school.

Pink has intimated that she, too, was the victim of abuse when she was younger, although she has refused to reveal whether it was of the emotional, physical or sexual variety, or indeed who was responsible. However, it was, she has admitted, the cause of her delinquent behaviour growing up.

"I was abused, I was angry, and so I rebelled... [But] I'm not talking about that," she told the *Mail On Sunday*'s *Live Night & Day* magazine. "Everyone is emotionally abused at some stage. As for the rest, no comment."

It remains one of the few occasions that Pink, one of the most outspoken, garrulous and candid pop stars on the planet, has refused to reveal all.

Whatever the details of this "abuse", there is a clear sense in which Pink's torment and all of her tribulations growing up didn't just fail to derail her; they provided her with a powerful determination to succeed and virtually kick-started the career of the teenager, who was practically a homeless tearaway by the time she was 16, who would regularly leave home, only for her father to have to find her.

More even than seeing close friends die terrible drug-related deaths, it was the prospect of losing control of her talent by disappearing down the same path that galvanised the young Pink and convinced her to kick her bad habits. Besides, she realised that, once she had a career in the music industry in her sights, nothing else came close in terms of highs.

"I took all [my] energy and threw it into music," she said. "Getting a record deal was a bigger kick than anything a drug had ever given me. I had all these things to say and I wanted to get them out there. I needed to be strong and focused, so that was it."

Under the influence of everyone from Bette Midler to Billy Joel, Madonna to Janis Joplin, Don McLean to rap rivals 2Pac and Notorious B.I.G., Pink had begun to express herself in song while still in her early teens; her lyrics evinced a troubled soul and caused her mother to later say of her initial efforts, "They were always very introspective. Some of them were very black, and very deep, almost worrisome."

Pink might have been a mass of issues and mess of personality crises, but she was able to hold it together sufficiently during her "problem years" to begin performing solo in Philadelphia clubs when she was 14. And she may have been the quintessential outsider, but she was able to find enough like-minded people at high school with whom to form bands.

Her first outfit was called Middleground; they may not have gained popularity beyond Doylestown, but they did have an ongoing rivalry with another local band, The Jetsists, which increased both groups' notoriety in the area, especially when they held a Battle of the Bands contest at a local café. Not long after the members of Middleground went their separate ways, Pink was spotted by an MCA talent scout while performing at Philadelphia's Club Fever. Pink joined a short-lived girl group called Basic Instinct before becoming part of Atlanta-based R&B trio Choice, singing with Sharon Flanagan and Chrissy

Conway of the Christian girl group ZOEgirl. They sent a copy of their first song, 'Key To My Heart', to LaFace Records in Atlanta, where head honcho LA Reid – one of the founding fathers, alongside production cohort Kenneth 'Babyface' Edmonds, of contemporary R&B via their swingbeat/New Jack Swing sound of the late-'80s – overheard it and arranged for the group to fly there so that he could watch them perform.

Impressed, Reid offered the girls a record deal, although, because the girls were under 18, they had to get their parents to co-sign the contract. Pink, Sharon and Chrissie, having relocated to Atlanta, proceeded to record an album, and although 'Key To My Heart' would appear on the soundtrack of the 1996 film Kazaam, the album was never released and the group disbanded.

But this wasn't the end of Pink's tenure with LaFace – she stayed on the label as a solo act, employing the nom de stage Pink. There, Daryl Simmons, a musician, songwriter and producer – and another key architect of modern R&B – encouraged her to sing backing vocals for the likes of Diana Ross and Tevin Campbell, the latter a key figure, along with Usher and Bobby Brown, in the annals of New Jack Swing.

In 1999, Pink made her official debut as a solo artiste with 'Gonna Make Ya Move (Don't Stop)', a house/trance number issued by Activ Records in the UK, where it reached number 196 on the singles chart in February 1999, remaining on the top 200 for one week. It was an inauspicious start to Pink's career, and it remains overlooked to this day, a hard-to-find record that has yet to appear on any Pink album.

It wasn't until the start of the new century that Pink opened her account as a serious solo contender when, in April 2000, LaFace Records issued the single 'There You Go'. The sleeve – featuring a head-shot of the singer with her cropped hair a dazzling neon-pink hue, and her shoulders showing that she was wearing a shiny black leather biker jacket – hinted at Pink's androgynous image: the figure staring balefully from the front cover of 'There You Go' looking like a futuristic robo-woman seems today like the missing link between Annie Lennox and new British synthpop diva La Roux.

The music, meanwhile, was a solid example of the polished, experimental-yet-commercial R&B, all skittering percussion, stop-start rhythms and staccato strings, being purveyed at the time by TLC (the acoustic guitar figure at the start was highly reminiscent of the latter's 'No Scrubs', the single taken from the trio's 1999 *Fanmail* album, which was executive produced by LA Reid and Babyface) as well as such single-name stars of contemporary female turn-of-the-century soul as Aaliyah, Kelis, Mýa, Monica and Brandy. As for Pink's vocals, they were – again, typical of the genre – smooth, lightly melismatic, and exhibited restrained passion.

Given that it was a song about a failed relationship in which the man wants Pink back, the video for 'There You Go' bore a suitably dramatic narrative: one of Pink's old boyfriends calls her up asking for a ride, and she reluctantly agrees to pick him up; cue our heroine arriving, on a sleek superbike, on the top of a building that overlooks her ex's apartment. She proceeds to call him on her mobile phone, then revs up her motorcycle, jumps off at the last minute and watches as the machine soars off the building and crashes into her ex's apartment window before exploding into flames.

Finally, Pink jumps in a car driven by her new squeeze and gives her hapless ex the finger as the two new lovebirds drive into the sunset. The none-too-subtle subtext: 'There You Go' marked the arrival of a ballsy, brazen new talent, one with whom it was best not to mess.

An impressive composition from the joint pens of Pink, Kandi Burruss and Kevin 'She'kspere' Briggs, the latter (who also produced the track) a seminal player, along with Timbaland, Rodney Jerkins and Dallas Austin, in modern R&B, 'There You Go' peaked at number seven on the US *Billboard* Top 100 and number six on the UK singles chart. Meanwhile in Australia, where Pink was hugely popular from the off (her next single, 'Most Girls', reached pole position there), the single was also a big hit, selling more than 70,000 copies, enough to earn it platinum status.

'There You Go' was the first single lifted from Pink's debut album *Can't Take Me Home*. Released in April 2000 by LaFace, *Can't Take Me Home* marked the start of Pink's career as a stratospherically successful singer and songwriter – of the 13 tracks, she co-wrote almost half – and the beginning and end of her brief career as an R&B act before her shift towards pop and rock with 2001's *M!ssundaztood* album. It also signalled the end of the idea of Pink as wannabe and second-stringer: in the summer of 2000, she was the opening act for US boyband 'N Sync on their American tour; thereafter, she would be top of the bill, and any support acts would be hers for the bidding.

Can't Take Me Home was produced by Babyface, She'kspere, Kandi Burruss, Terence 'Tramp Baby' Abney (who also played keyboards and programmed the machine rhythms), Daryl Simmons and Tricky Stewart (not to be confused with the British trip-hop pioneer, Tricky). It achieved considerable success, going double platinum in the States, where it peaked at number 26 and sold over two million copies – worldwide, five million units in total were shifted.

The album bequeathed two US Top 10 singles – 'There You Go' and 'Most Girls' – and a third, 'You Make Me Sick', which entered the US Top 40 and the UK Top 10 (it also featured in the film *Save The Last Dance*, while album opener 'Split Personality' appeared on the soundtrack to the 2001 children's movie, *The Princess Diaries*).

Reviews of *Can't Take Me Home* were mainly complimentary. There were positive comments for the glistening, "bling" production, the detailed intricacy of the arrangements, the layered drum patterns and the sultry slow grooves. There was acclaim for the well-crafted songs, even if they were, as one writer noted, "More ingratiating than immediate, and if dance-pop should be anything, it should be indelible upon at least the second listen, if not the first. Many of the songs on *Can't Take Me Home* need a few spins before they truly sink in." And most writers admired Pink's singing. It was, some suggested, a tad characterless, a function, perhaps, of the machine-soul milieu as much as anything. Others noted the way she held back from over-singing and over-emoting, although one tartly remarked on her similarity to other R&B divas: "She makes a pretty good Monica, but we already have one of those."

Some write-ups pointed out the similarities between Pink's debut and much of the black dance music recorded in the wake of TLC's *Fanmail*, R&B singer Aaliyah's groundbreaking work in the mid-'90s with Tim 'Timbaland' Mosley, the producer who set soul music onto unforeseen paths and gave female soul a hi-tech facelift ahead of the 21st century, and the similarly innovative efforts of The Neptunes (the production squad comprising Pharrell Williams and Chad Hugo) with their own protégée, singer Kelis. "If *Can't Take Me Home* pales next to *Fanmail*, it's not Pink's fault, nor is it because the album is sub-par; it's simply because it follows in the footsteps of a record that's as close to a modern classic as contemporary soul gets," wrote one reviewer, while the man from *Rolling Stone* opined that, "Every melismatic groan, every clipped harmony, every post-Timbaland beat, every synth setting – like the 'No Scrubs'-style harpsichord – is copped from some R&B hit of the last 18 months. And the fiery internal dialogue of 'Split Personality' would have seemed more original before Kelis' 'Caught Out There'."

Although *Can't Take Me Home* is today seen as, at best, a promising first stop on the way towards the success Pink achieved with the crossover pop-rock of her *M!ssundaztood* album, it is actually a sterling collection of shiny urban contemporary pop, even if, notwithstanding a certain grittiness to her vocal timbre, she sounds little like the snarly brat-punk we know and love today. It starts with the typically jerky 'Split Personality', on which Pink displays a vocal maturity uncanny for a 20-year-old arriviste, as she effortlessly flits between octaves a la Christina (Xtina) Aguilera, that other dazzling young mistress of the R&B melisma. 'Hell Wit Ya' is propelled by a startling electro-bass pattern like the rapid-fire rat-a-tat of a computer-game gun and, with its swear words, posits Pink as a sort of X-Rated Xtina or Bad-Girl Britney (Spears). 'Most Girls', a mid-tempo number featuring the R&B-ubiquitous harpsichord, is another statement of intent asserting Pink's independence and self-sufficiency, her eschewing of conventional romance mores and sexual roles, and distaste for "bling" – "I never cared too much for love, it was all a bunch of mush"…"I'm not every girl and I don't need that world to validate me."

'There You Go' was an obvious choice for single, and carries much the same message as Destiny's Child's 2001 single 'Independent Women' (although Beyoncé and Co's seminal girl group had begun working with She'kspere and Rodney Jerkins on their own version of modern R&B back in 1998). 'You Make Me Sick' was formulaic but rife with enough hooks and double entendres to be considered as the third single from the album. 'Let Me Let You Know', 'Stop Falling', 'Do What U Do', 'Is It Love' and 'Love Is Such A Crazy Thing' were saved from ballad-ordinaire status by the fabulous production, notably the startling synthbass sound that appears throughout the latter like something from an old acid house track.

But the standout song on Pink's debut album was the title track, a mini-masterpiece of dubby space-disco and skittering post-jungle rhythms. The image of love as disease is worthy of Elvis Costello at his self-loathing peak while Pink presents herself as a supremely self-assured young woman: "You should have thought about that before you fucked with me," she sings, even though the expletive is deleted. It climaxes with her declaring, "It's a Pink thing," the artist as the centre of her own universe, harmonising with herself, via the wonders of multi-tracking, like a sassy, solipsist 21st century Supremes. It is the dazzling centrepiece of a superb first album of polished night-club pop.

Can't Take You Home unveiled an exciting new talent, placing Pink assuredly on the world's stage, the first step on the way towards her selling upwards of 30 million albums worldwide and becoming one of the biggest pop stars on the planet.

It would have been hard to believe, had it been divulged, that barely five years before, she was lying face down in a disco, waiting to die after a night of narcotic overindulgence. Because in 2000, Pink was the epitome of positive thinking and self-control, and only a fool would have bet against her being able to sustain it throughout the decade.

In August that year, 'Most Girls' became the second single to be released from her debut album. It peaked at number four on *Billboard*'s Hot 100 Singles Chart and was certified platinum. It was Pink's highest charting hit in the USA as a solo artist, tied with 'Get The Party Started', until her 2008 single 'So What' reached number one on *Billboard*'s Hot 100. It is also one of Pink's biggest hits in Australia, where it peaked at number one and was certified platinum. 'You Make Me Sick' was the third and last single from *Can't Take Me Home*. It peaked at number 33 on the *Billboard* Hot 100 and reached number nine in the UK. The single, which got mixed reviews, failed to become as omnipresent a radio staple as her previous two (one reviewer opined that its release was tantamount to commercial suicide and predicted that it would bomb disastrously), and yet it still managed to reach the Top 10 in January 2001 in the UK, where it was Pink's third consecutive singles chart entry. The video for the song, featuring Pink in a variety of poses – sitting on Santa's knee, smothered by petals à la *American Beauty* – was filmed the week before her visit to Australia in late 2000 and was directed by Dave Meyers, who she had collaborated with twice previously on her first two singles from *Can't Take Me Home*. Although it didn't do as well as its predecessors in Australia and peaked at 25, it managed to sell over 35,000 copies there and was accredited gold.

Despite providing a substantial stepping-stone to success, Pink has subsequently all but disowned *Can't Take Me Home*, dismissing it as the work of her producers, as a triumph of marketing, and not the autonomous first salvo she would have liked it to have been.

"LA Reid pretty much put together my first album," she told *Bang* magazine. "I didn't have much say; I didn't have much power." Trouble was, Pink felt it wasn't really representative of who she was. "I like it and I hate it," she says of her debut album. "That period was so fucked."

Amazingly, given what we know about Pink the

super-strong woman, around the release of her first album she was being encouraged to take etiquette classes and have media training. But she rebelled against such attempts at contrivance.

"They used my personality as my marketing, but not before they had wanted me to take etiquette classes, media coaching, all that shit," she told the *Observer Magazine*. "I said 'no' to etiquette classes because that was an insult to my mother," she said. "I did media coaching, but the guy left. He said, 'I can't help her.' They wanted to teach me to be diplomatic, to give journalists the answers they want, and I'm like, 'Wouldn't you rather have the truth?' The only thing I know how to say is what I feel."

It wouldn't be too long before she would throw off her shackles and reveal to the world the real Pink.

Chapter 2

Hit And M!ss

"All the girls that came out in the last couple of years, we all got thrown into one bucket. I don't want people to throw me in that bucket."

If Pink's intention was to separate herself from the femme-pop pack, to differentiate herself and prove her uniqueness, she ironically achieved just that with a single that saw her singing alongside three of her peers.

In April 2001, she recorded a cover of Labelle's 1975 smash hit 'Lady Marmalade' with Christina Aguilera (of whom she would later be critical in the press), rapper Lil' Kim and R&B girl Mýa for the soundtrack of the film *Moulin Rouge!* An early disco hit, the song was written by Bob Crewe (who co-wrote many of the hits recorded by The Four Seasons) and Kenny Nolan; the pair had previously collaborated on the hit Frankie Valli ballad 'My Eyes Adored You'. It is most famous for its sexually suggestive chorus of "voulez-vous coucher avec moi (ce soir)?" – which, when Leona Lewis sang it on TV talent show *The X Factor*, saw the lyric changed to "voulez-vous chanter avec moi (ce soir)?" – although, needless to say, Pink et al's version featured the unexpurgated original line.

Produced by hip hoppers Rockwilder and Missy Elliott (who also made an MC cameo appearance on the track's intro and outro), this new version of 'Lady Marmalade', despite coming out only three years after a cover by British girl group All Saints, topped the charts in 15 countries, including New Zealand, Britain, Australia and the US, where it stayed at number one on the *Billboard* Hot 100 for five weeks, from May 26 to June 30, 2001.

Helped by the high-energy production and the four singers' virtuoso performances (well, three – Lil' Kim's contribution was a rap), it became the most successful airplay-only single ever (it was only the second song in *Billboard* chart history, after Aaliyah's 2000 single 'Try Again', to reach number one without being released in a major commercially available single format such as a CD or CD maxi single). It was Aguilera's fourth US number one single and the first time at pole position for Kim, Pink and Mýa in the US. It remained in the Stateside Top 40 for 17 weeks and became the best-selling single for each of the artists involved except for Christina Aguilera and Pink.

The success of 'Lady Marmalade' received a further boost from its accompanying music video, which featured the girls in a variety of lingerie, basques and fishnet stockings. Directed by Paul Hunter and filmed at the end of March 2001 on sets (in Los Angeles) built to resemble the actual Moulin Rouge nightclub around the turn of the century (1890-1910), it would go on to win MTV Video Music awards for Best Video of the Year and Best Video from a Film and receive nominations for Best Dance Video, Best Pop Video, Best

Choreography (for Tina Landon), and Best Art Direction. The song itself won a 2002 Grammy Award in the category of Best Pop Collaboration with Vocals and considerably increased the international profile of the four performers.

Pink acquitted herself well on the song and in the video, and her performances in both instances were sassy and assured, but they didn't necessarily realise her ambition to distance herself from her contemporaries. Angered by comparisons to the pop and R&B female singers of the day, and fearing assumptions that she was merely the dance-pop creation of her producers and label-owners, she was determined to prove her worth, and for her "for real" credentials to be writ large, on her next release.

To help her achieve her aim and facilitate her struggle for artistic control and concomitant transition from R&B puppet to fully fledged, autonomous, all-snarling pop-rock crossover monster, Pink needed the right collaborator. And she already had somebody in mind: Linda Perry, lesbian singer with half-forgotten '90s alternative rock band 4 Non Blondes, who would, on the back of her success with Pink, go on to become a superstar writer-producer gun-for-hire for the likes of Christina Aguilera, Gwen Stefani and Alicia Keys.

According to Pink in VH1's *Driven* she first got in touch with Perry, one of her teenage idols, by leaving a message on her answering machine after finding her number in her make-up artist's phone book. She explained that she wanted to write with her and have her help with production on her forthcoming second album. She added that the reason she wanted to work with Perry was that 4 Non Blondes' 1992 album, *Bigger, Better, Faster, More!*, was one of her favourites when she was growing up.

Later, she described the way she had made contact with

Perry, and joked that it had more sinister undertones, comparing it to stalking. She explained that, instead of just leaving messages on her answer-phone, she would sing 4 Non Blondes songs back to her. Eventually, Perry cracked. "You're fucking crazy," she apparently told Pink. "Come on over."

Perry was now on board for songwriting and production duties – with assistance in the studio from Dallas Austin and Scott Storch, the Canadian hip hop producer responsible for hits for 50 Cent, Busta Rhymes, Ice Cube and many more. In a further bid to change people's perceptions of her, Pink also recruited hard rockers Steven Tyler of Aerosmith and Richie Sambora of Bon Jovi to make guest appearances on a couple of tracks. Now all that Pink needed to do was convince her label boss, LA Reid, that her new, rockier direction was a good idea.

During the making of her second album, she told *Bang* magazine, she fought with Reid "tooth and nail". "I was like, 'This is what I wanna do – you gotta believe in me, and send me back to McDonalds if you don't,'" she said. "And there was a struggle and it was a fight, but me and LA's fights are fun because a) I always win, Ha! and b) he's passionate and he's musical and he supports me and he believes in me, so he gave me the opportunity to fail."

"Failure" is hardly a word you can reasonably associate with Pink's sophomore release. Released in November 2001, *M!ssundaztood* – so-titled because of her belief that that's what she was; that people had a false image of her – was certified gold or platinum in more than 20 countries (although it only reached the top spot in Ireland). It has sold anywhere between 12 and 16 million copies, spawning the hits 'Get The Party Started', 'Just Like A Pill', 'Family Portrait' and 'Don't Let Me Get Me'. The lead single, 'Get The Party Started' (written and produced by Perry), went top five in the US and elsewhere, and number one in Australia. The album's other singles – 'Don't Let Me Get Me', and the Dallas Austin-produced 'Just Like A Pill' and 'Family Portrait' – were also radio and chart successes, with 'Just Like A Pill' becoming Pink's first solo number one hit in the UK. There *M!ssundaztood* was the second-best-selling album of 2002 (it has since sold 1.8 million copies, received a six times platinum certification and now ranks 94th on the Official UK Charts Company's all-time best-selling albums list).

M!ssundaztood and 'Get The Party Started' earned nominations at the 2003 Grammy Awards for Best Pop Vocal Album and Best Female Pop Vocal Performance, while at the 2002 MTV Video Music Awards, the video for '...Party Started' won in the categories of Best Female Video and Best Dance Video.

And it all started, all of the awards and number one global smash hits, with a simple request from Perry to Pink to bare her soul.

"In the beginning I just said: 'What do you feel?'" Perry said at the time, "and she [Pink] would just sit behind the piano and sing". During the writing and recording of the album, Pink actually moved into Perry's Los Angeles home, where the pair spent several months writing songs and kicking around ideas.

Those four simple words – "what do you feel?" – encouraged Pink to pour her heart out in song. Eventually, with Perry at her side, she came up with eight tracks – more than half the album: 'M!ssundaztood', 'Get The Party Started', 'Respect', 'Dear Diary', 'Eventually', 'Lonely Girl' (which featured Linda Perry on vocals), 'Gone To California' and 'My Vietnam'. With those eight songs, Pink managed to radically alter her audience's perception of her as an artist and as a woman.

This is hardly surprising considering the subjects that she addressed in those songs. On 'Don't Let Me Get Me' she paints a picture of herself as the definitive bad girl – her socks are dirty, her parents hate her – then she sings, "I'm a hazard to myself... I'm my own worst enemy", before declaring, "I wanna be somebody else." She references LA Reid and makes plain her intention not to be marketed as a clean-cut popette because "all you have to change is everything you are". Even the biggest teen-pop diva on the planet at that time makes a cameo appearance: "Tired of being compared to damn Britney Spears," complains Pink of her so-called rival. "She's so pretty/That just ain't me." (Later, she was able to empathise with Spears when she fell from grace and became, like Pink, a "bad girl": "I've always loved Britney," she said in 2006. "I'm her friend in public and in private. I have always defended her. She's a nice girl and she's getting a bad press. I feel sorry for her.")

On 'Just Like A Pill' she alludes to her drug abuse as a teenager and uses narcotics as a metaphor for unhealthy relationships. She addresses her father's war experiences in 'My Vietnam' (towards the end there is a burst of Jimi Hendrix's 'Star Spangled Banner', a favourite of US soldiers on the front line in Vietnam) and uses the image of battle as a metaphor for her turbulent upbringing, extending her own idea of herself as a "walking conflict": "Mother was a lunatic, she liked to push my buttons... Never liked school that much... They keep dropping bombs and I keep score".

'Family Portrait' delves even further into Pink's background and shines a light on the darkest corners of her dysfunctional family, her parents' divorce and the destruction it wreaked. "Mama, please stop cryin'... your pain is painful... I told daddy you didn't mean those nasty things you said... It ain't easy

Pink photographed for *The Face*, June 2002. (LEE JENKINS/CORBIS OUTLINE)

Pink on stage, circa 2000. (CHRISTINA RADISH/REDFERNS)

The 2001 'Lady Marmalade' video shoot. Left to right: Lil' Kim, Pink, Mya, & Christina Aguilera. (KEVIN MAZUR/WIREIMAGE)

Pink and Bally Total Fitness Health Clubs launch a nationwide dance exercise class based on the moves of the singer, 2002. (BOB RIHA JR/GETTYIMAGES)

Pink's video shoot for 'Get This Party Started', October 2001. (ARNOLD TURNER/WIREIMAGE)

Pink and mom Judy Moore at the Beacon Theatre in New York City, May 2002. (KEVIN MAZUR/WIREIMAGE)

Pink, Lisa Marie Presley and Avril Lavigne
backstage at the MTV Video Music Awards, 2002.
(PHOTO BY KMAZUR/WIREIMAGE)

Pink performing on *Top Of The Pops*, BBC TV studios,
London 2002. (MARK ALLAN/WIREIMAGE)

Pink filming the video for 'Feel Good Time' which
featured in the movie *Charlie's Angel 2:
Full Throttle*, May 2003. (THEO WARGO/WIREIMAGE)

At the Brit Awards at London's Earls Court,
February 20, 2003. (DAVE HOGAN/GETTY IMAGES)

Pink takes the stage in a Red Bull Formula One car before performing during the Red Bull Racing Formula One Team launch at Melbourne Docklands, March 2005, in Australia. (RYAN PIERSE/GETTY IMAGES)

Pink donates a cheque to the Breast Cancer Research Fundraiser in New York City, September 2005. (ANDREW H. WALKER/GETTY IMAGES)

Pamela Anderson and Pink attend PETA's 25th Anniversary Gala and Humanitarian Awards Show, Paramount Studios, Los Angeles, 2005. (MICHAEL CAULFIELD/WIREIMAGE)

James T Moore, Pink's father and Pink, in 2006. (KEVIN MAZUR/WIREIMAGE)

Pink performs at the secret album launch party, performing songs from *I'm Not Dead* at Lock 17, March 2006 in London. (DAVE HOGAN/GETTY IMAGES)

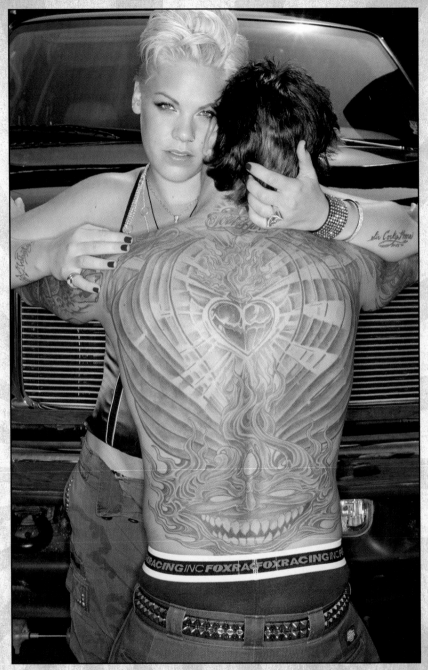

Pink and Carey Hart. (GEORGE HOLZ/CONTOURPHOTOS.COM)

growing up in World War 3..." It works both as an unwavering account of family strife in general, but also as a coruscating example of rock autobiography, to the extent that Pink's family were devastated when they heard the song.

"It hurt the whole family, but it swept everything up and we were better for it," she said, although her mother was most hurt by the line in 'My Vietnam' about her being 'a lunatic': "My mum was really angry for a while. [But] we've worked out all our issues. I don't like to sweep shit under a rug – just call a spade a spade and deal with it." Besides, as she explained in the *Sun* newspaper in 2008, it is her very forthrightness and refusal, from *M!ssundaztood* onwards, to flinch from the truth that have made people find real value in her work.

"I got a letter from this 13-year-old girl saying her grandfather was raping her mother. It went on saying her mother had died and now he was raping her. She said when she listened to my music she knew she didn't want to die. She wrote saying I should never stop making music because it helped her."

Later, she said of 'Family Portrait': "That song kills me still. It's the most honest thing I've ever written and it is the one song that has connected me to so many other young people who have gone, or are going through, that whole painful process. That's the one thing that makes it all worthwhile."

The songs that Pink co-wrote with Linda Perry – 'Family Portrait', 'Just Like A Pill', 'My Vietnam' and 'Don't Let Me Get Me' as well as 'Dear Diary' ("I've been a bad girl for so long"), 'Eventually' ("This life is lonely when everybody wants something"), 'Lonely Girl' ("I can remember the very first time I cried") and 'Gone To California' (where she leaves for the West Coast because the "city of brotherly love" – her home city of Philadelphia – "is full of pain and hurt") were full of empathy for suffering souls and insights into the dark side of the human condition. More than anything, on these songs Pink faced her own demons head-on, disclosing the details of her troubled past with alarming frankness.

For this reason, *M!ssundaztood* has been described as "the teen-pop *In Utero*", a reference to the Nirvana album made prior to the suicide of Kurt Cobain. As a slice of musical therapy and self-analysis, as the work of an artist rejecting her past and coming of age, it could also be compared to *Jagged Little Pill*, the album that Alanis Morissette made as she emerged from a period as a manufactured popster. Indeed, *Entertainment Weekly* wrote that "Pink captures girlie confusion with greater accuracy, and delight, than Alanis Morissette."

Robert Christgau, the self-styled "Dean of US rock critics", described the songs on *M!ssundaztood* as "confessional, dark, downtempo – and, OK, a little gauche sometimes, which just makes them seem realer. Despite Pink's audacious claim that she's not as pretty as 'damn Britney Spears', celebrity anxiety takes a backseat to a credible personal pain rooted in credible family travails, a pain held at bay by expression."

It wasn't all downbeat dirge-rock, however. The strength of *M!ssundaztood* is that, although most of its songs are rooted in real experience, particularly the suffering that Pink endured as a child from a broken home, distressing memories didn't stop her from making it all accessible and enjoyable for the listener at all points. The album is a melodic delight from beginning to end. 'Get The Party Started', also co-written with Perry, is the perfect album opener and as much of a perennial dancefloor-filler as Cyndi Lauper's 'Girls Just Want To Have Fun'. '18 Wheeler' is swaggering redneck rock – you can hear from this track why Pink was mooted for the lead role in a biopic of the legendary Janis Joplin (the original version of the track featured numerous expletives, but they were deleted in order to avoid a Parental Advisory sticker, because that may have harmed sales. No uncensored versions of '18 Wheeler' exist, but Pink performs a non-bowdlerised version on tour). The title track is another mid-paced party-starter. 'Numb' does indeed bear more than a passing resemblance to Nirvana's epochal grunge metal. 'Misery' is a gritty blast of good-time blues-rock that sees Pink matching Aerosmith's Steven Tyler note for gruff note. And 'Respect' disses boys at a tempo you can dance to.

M!ssundaztood was a bewildering amalgam of sounds and styles that shouldn't have fit together, but defied all odds and did. It bubbled over with imagination, as hooky pop songs rubbed shoulders with glitzy dancefloor anthems, lighters-aloft stadium ballads with lite metal. The production brought rock grit, soul gloss and a hip hop snap to bear on proceedings, and managed to turn an incredibly diverse range of songs into a coherent collection. It was a triumph for Perry, who coaxed out of Pink a series of performances that were raw and heart-felt but bristling with energy and the sort of emoting that was infectious. And it was a triumph for Pink, who could easily have coasted along the R&B route but felt that it was unrepresentative of the real her.

As one reviewer noted, "There hasn't been a record in the mainstream this vibrant or this alive in a long, long time." Even *Spin* magazine's Rob Sheffield, who was less impressed, preferring "the lively R&B beats of *Can't Take Me Home*" to what he considered to be "traditionalist rock clichés such as 'Misery', which sounds like The Black Crowes, which couldn't have been the idea", he was forced to acknowledge that "Pink deserves respect for expressing herself instead of going through the teen-pop motions – even if her execution isn't up to her ambitions."

The singles released from *M!ssundaztood* helped spread the word that Pink had undergone a dramatic transformation. 'Get The Party Started' was first: released in October 2001 in the United States and January 2002 in Britain, it peaked at number four in the States – becoming Pink's second biggest solo hit there alongside 'Most Girls' (2000) and 'So What' (2008) – and number two in the UK, where it was just kept off the top spot by the posthumous release of 'My Sweet Lord' by George Harrison, who died in November 2001. During recording of the song, Pink apparently learned how to programme drums and even played the bass. By revelling in the experimental, anything-goes atmosphere, she and Perry created a nightclub classic. "You create something in your bedroom or your house, and it's just a fun thing that you're doing," Pink said. "Then all of a sudden, you hear that song that you started in your house, and it's on the radio. And people are now acknowledging it. It's just trippy."

One of Pink's signature anthems, 'Get The Party Started' attracted numerous covers. There were punk versions, synth-pop versions, acoustic troubadour versions, hardcore techno versions, Chinese pop versions, even a version by Dame Shirley Bassey recorded for a spy-themed 2006 Marks & Spencer Christmas TV advertising campaign that the *Guardian* noted had "a grand, imperious swoop worthy of a Bond theme."

'Get The Party Started' was nominated for a Grammy Award in 2003 in the category of Best Female Pop Vocal Performance, (it lost to Norah Jones' 'Don't Know Why'). Upbeat and supremely infectious, it won the award for Favourite Song at the Kids' Choice Awards of 2002, and at the MTV Europe Music Awards of 2002 it won the award for Best Song.

The music video, which itself was nominated at the 2002 MTV Video Music Awards for Best Pop Video and won the awards for Best Female Video and Best Dance Video, was shot by director Dave Meyers in Los Angeles in late September 2001. It has a fun-time storyline in which Pink and a friend steal two skateboards from two boys, get into a club without paying via an open window and once inside dance with a certain Kevin Federline, who later married Britney Spears.

'Don't Let Me Get Me', written by Pink and Dallas Austin, was the album's second single in February 2002. It reached number six in the UK charts and number eight in the States. The video found her fighting with LA Reid, with stylists, even with herself in the mirror of a locker room. But the next two singles lifted from *M!ssundaztood* had more of an impact and were accompanied by more memorable clips.

'Just like A Pill', the third single in June 2002 and another Pink/Dallas Austin co-write, reached number eight in the US and became Pink's first UK number one single. The video, directed by Francis Lawrence (who went on to direct the Will Smith movie *I Am Legend*), was something of a departure from previous Pink videos. Darker, and featuring the singer dressed in black, and with black hair (with pink streaks, natch) throughout, it showed her lip-synching the song in front of hordes of goth-lite revellers as well as an elephant.

Pink's encounter with this largest of land animals during filming was to have a profound effect on her, alerting her for the first time to the plight of animals in captivity. "Pink learned about the abuse of captive elephants when a trainer brought one onto the set of the video," said a spokesman for PETA (People for the Ethical Treatment of Animals). "She could see that something was wrong and she called us to learn more about the issue." It was after filming the 'Just Like A Pill' video that she became an active campaigner on behalf of PETA.

'Family Portrait', written by Pink and Scott Storch, was the final single issued from *M!ssundaztood* in December 2002 in

North America and January 2003 in Europe. The song peaked at number 20 in the US and number 11 in the UK. The video is a poignant, darkly shot affair starring Pink and an identically dressed young girl in vest and tracksuit bottoms, presumably playing the young Pink torn apart by the divorce of her parents. The image of the girl lip-synching the lyrics, particularly the part about not wanting to have to split the holidays or have two separate addresses, is quite heartrending. At the end of the video, the girl disappears into the TV screen in Pink's front room to join a "normal" suburban nuclear family, with a loving, smiling and patently not arguing mother and father, brother and sister, all happily sitting around the table of a brightly coloured kitchen.

As far as Pink was concerned, the video was yet another exercise in self-healing, for herself as well as for her fans.

"Music's like group therapy," she told *Look* magazine in 2008. "I was so miserable about talking about personal stuff, then I started getting letters from girls saying, 'Me and my mom are talking again because of that song.' So I made a promise to continue being honest at whatever cost." She explained that she was so overwhelmed by people interrogating her about her own family history as a result of the 'Family Portrait' song and video that, at one point, she burst into tears and stormed out of the interview. But she soon saw the error of her ways, and the validity of her honesty, when yet more letters began pouring in.

"I said, 'Fuck this, I'm not doing this anymore.' But then all the letters started coming in and it just became so worth it. It's like seriously, letters from 'You helped me to come out' to 'My boyfriend was abusive.' Literally, I get letters like this all the time. One trumps the next with tragedy and these are the kinds of people getting something from me wearing my heart on my sleeve. So fuck me, and fuck what I think about it."

Chapter 3

Save My Life

"I was going: 'You want a record? Fine, I'll write 10 songs in a week for your fuckin' record and you can press it up and put it out.'"

Pink was, after the staggering success of *M!ssundaztood*, entering that rarefied realm inhabited by only the world's biggest stars. It was the kind of success she had always hoped for, the kind she'd been working for since she was 15. But there was a downside to having such a massively successful, globally popular album, namely the what-do-I-do-for-an-encore? syndrome. Because, like Michael Jackson after *Thriller*, Madonna after *Like A Virgin* and Prince after *Purple Rain*, she now had an almighty obstacle to overcome: she had to do it all over again. Not surprisingly, there were times, in the wake of *M!ssundaztood*, when the pressures of fame and the responsibilities that come with it got to Pink.

As she admitted in an interview with *The Irish Times* in

2006, she wasn't happy with the way her record company wanted her to make an album so swiftly on the heels of *M!ssundaztood*.

"I was kind of rebelling against the label on that one," she said. "I was going: 'You want a record? Fine, I'll write 10 songs in a week for your fuckin' record and you can press it up and put it out.'"

By all accounts, during the promotion of *M!ssundaztood*, Pink was very emotional, feeling weighed down by the sense of obligation and duty to perform, in more ways than one. "That was an awful time," she said. "I was walking out of half my interviews, crying. I just felt they were putting a quarter in the slot to watch the monkey dance."

And yet, within six months of 'Family Portrait', the last single from *M!ssundaztood*, coming out, she was back working on new material for a third Pink album. In mid-2003, she contributed the song 'Feel Good Time' to the soundtrack of the film *Charlie's Angels: Full Throttle*. She even found time to make a cameo appearance as a motocross race ramp owner/promoter in the movie, which she described as "a blast". During the same period, a song Pink co-wrote with Damon Elliott, the record producer son of Dionne Warwick, was released on her 'Lady Marmalade' mate Mýa's album *Moodring*.

'Feel Good Time' was co-written by singer Beck, produced by electronic music artist William Orbit and based on a sample of 'Fresh Garbage', the opening track from the eponymous 1968 debut album by cult late-'60s psychedelic jazz-rock fusion band Spirit, whose brilliant lead singer and guitarist, Randy California, had once jammed with Jimi Hendrix. It became Pink's first single to miss the Top 40 on *Billboard*'s Hot 100 chart (it peaked at number 60), although it was a hit in Europe and Australia, reaching number three in the UK. It was also nominated for the 2004 Grammy Award in the Best Pop Collaboration With Vocals category. 'Feel Good Time' was a great single, not least because of the unexpected decision to use a Spirit sample instead of a more predictable choice from the '60s or '70s soul/R&B pantheon. Interestingly, Beck and sometime techno producer William Orbit's song was initially designed to be recorded by Beck himself, but after Pink expressed a desire to cover it, he gave the song to her, and Beck's vocals and guitar were removed and replaced with Pink's own voice (Beck's original version was played on Orbit's radio show and, while never officially released, can be found on file-sharing programmes).

The relative commercial failure of 'Feel Good Time', far from putting Pink off the process of writing and recording, seemed to spur Pink into action. No sooner had she completed the single than she started thinking about her next batch of tunes. The question was: who to collaborate with this time? Linda Perry had proven the right choice, and then some, for *M!ssundaztood*. But maybe it was a case of, "Been there, done that." Or perhaps the experience was too heavy to be repeated so soon: "When we write our songs together," Pink said, "we're like two thunderstorms colliding. It can be good or it can be really bad. It's intense."

For whatever reasons, Perry contributed only three songs to Pink's third album, *Try This*. The bulk of the material was co-written with Tim Armstrong, the singer with American punk band Rancid, whom Pink had met through a mutual friend at a video shoot for punk/hip hop supergroup Transplants. Pink and Armstrong hit it off immediately and Pink ended up co-writing 10 songs with him in a week when Rancid were on a tour with The Foo Fighters. Eight of these tracks appeared on *Try This*. The album also included a collab-

oration with ultra-hip, sexually experimental and highly con-
frontational electroclash artist Peaches (née Merrill Nisker)
called 'Oh My God'.

According to Pink, the sessions at her home studio with
Damon Elliott, Peaches and Linda Perry were going well
enough. But it was when she and Armstrong got together that
creative sparks began to fly. She knew there would be magic
and mayhem the minute they met at that video shoot.

Pink later recalled their initial encounter: "He said, 'I have
some songs for you. It's gonna be amazing.'" Pink, an old
Rancid fan, replied: "You wanna work with me? Wow!"

Travis Barker, drummer with Blink 182 and Transplants, as
well as fellow Rancid members Matt Freeman and Lars
Frederiksen, were also on hand as Pink and Armstrong worked
on tracks, which made the process even more of a breeze.

"Working with Tim and Travis Barker was really fast, really
easy," she said. "There was no resistance with this album.
Making *M!ssundaztood* was almost too much; it's emotionally
draining to be that naked and that vulnerable. I just knew I
wanted to have fun and I didn't want to complain all the time.
I wanted to stop whining and start wailing."

There is plenty of wailing – and roaring, and snarling, and
growling – on *Try This*. It is a less angst-ridden collection than
its predecessor. She appears more content, happy in her state of
snotty fury, railing against all manner of anonymous irritants,
straights, losers and villains who dare get in her way. Her message, as the sleevenotes for her album had it, was simple:
"Embrace the freak that you are."

What, asked the journalist from *Q* magazine sent along to
interview Pink around the release of *Try This*, do people expect
when they meet her?

"They expect me to be a monster," she replied. "People have

told me they were scared to meet me, like, 'I thought you were going to rip my head off.'"

"You certainly have an image," parried the man from *Q*. Pink liked that.

"I guess," she said. "Do I? Like hard-partying? Angry?"

"Not quite," teased the journalist. "You're quite girl-next-door, really."

For once, Pink was speechless.

"Really?" she said, stunned. "I've never, ever, ever in my life been told that until today. Where the fuck do you live?"

Of all the dance-pop/teen pop singers to emerge in 1999, more than Britney Spears or Christina Aguilera, Pink seemed to be enjoying the most solid, album-based career. If it did anything, it confirmed what we suspected from her first two albums: that, whereas Britney and Xtina were R&B girls and disco divas, working with The Neptunes or whoever the latest hip-hop whiz happened to be, Pink was a closet metalhead and grunge kid, just waiting for her inner punk to be unleashed.

And she was a punk, if by "punk" you mean someone prepared to challenge themselves and those around them. In her own way, Pink was as punk as the bands who passed for punk around the time of the release of *Try This* – bands such as Green Day. If punk's fundamental credo was "rip it up and start again", she followed it to the letter: a white R&B singer at a time when black radio had closed its doors to white artists, she turned her back on that world, going rock'n'roll with Dallas Austin, a mainstream R&B producer, and Linda Perry, a lesbian rocker dismissed as a has-been when her group 4 Non Blondes split. Pink's multiplatinum 2001 breakthrough, *M!ssundaztood*, was an audacious makeover – not so much because of the switch in musical styles but because it saw Pink, frustrated by where she was, abandon the shallow concerns of her early work for a lyrical and musical depth that pop ordinarily denies.

But Pink is no fool, and she was careful not to alienate her first fans; rather she kept them on-board while attracting legions of converts. She had found – created – a useful niche: outrageous enough to appeal to Courtney Love fans, but cute enough to appeal to kids. Her music, post-*M!ssundaztood*, reflected the broad appeal of her "image"; an original, dynamic sound culled from seemingly contradictory sources, a smooth blend of hard rock riffs, R&B rhythms and pop melodies, and a confessional singer-songwriter's approach to soul-baring. If it was a surprise that Pink had an album like *M!ssundaztood* in her, it was perhaps even more surprising that, with *Try This*, she was able to pull off the same trick twice — and to do so with completely different, but equally unlikely, collaborators.

The personnel on *Try This* included Pink on lead vocals, Tim Armstrong on guitar, acoustic bass, keyboards, backup vocals, loops and sound effects (he also did some engineering and production), Jonathan Davis on guitar, acoustic guitar, bass, drum programming and keyboards, Linda Perry on guitar, sitar, mellotron and production and Damon Elliott handling percussion, keyboards, programming and production. In addition, there were, as part of the *Try This* musical mix, organ, synthesiser, glockenspiel, turntables, trombone, trumpet, baritone sax, violin, and something called an Omnichord. There were three people alone involved in the photography and art direction of the CD jacket; Pink appeared on the front, back and inner sleeve in a variety of poses: smoking, scowling, screaming, tied to a post, but always in black and in various states of undress.

But, although Pink has always been big on image, despite protestations that she's no over-made-up girlie mannequin, it was really the music that mattered most. Of the tracks that were not written with either Armstrong or Perry, 'God Is A DJ' – which portrays Pink as the girl with her skirt pulled high and her middle finger in the air, the sort of rebellion-lite that is again redolent of Alanis Morissette circa *Jagged Little Pill* – was a guitar-led rocker penned by Pink with Billy Mann and Jonathan Davis, while 'Love Song', a co-write with Damon Elliott, provides the album with an effective, quietly dramatic closer.

Of the three tracks written and recorded with Linda Perry, 'Try Too Hard' is straight-up riff rock that sees Pink, or at least the protagonist of the song, take on a wannabe who tries to be "different" by copying the right people, possibly a dig at fellow Perry collaborator Christina Aguilera or punk-pop labelmate Avril Lavigne. "People like that make her sick, she yells, complaining that she's surrounded by them everywhere she looks, but she might as well yawn, so unimpressed is she by this imaginary rival who does what the title of the song says. 'Waiting For Love', the second Perry team-up, is a semi-acoustic, mid-tempo rock ballad that, halfway through, flicks the switch to balls-out-rock, then spends the duration veering between both modes, all the while electronic FX and electric guitar squeals vying for space in the mix. It's a bit of a mess of ideas, but it probably gets the party started. 'Catch Me While I'm Sleeping' is simply stunning, and a total departure for the Pink-Perry partnership. A languid ballad featuring sitar, strings, an insistent beat and alternately whispered and violently sensual vocals, it recalls the mid-'70s ornate soul of Thom Bell, the sort of sumptuous but light and airy R&B that, if Prince were to have written it, would be hailed as a massive return to form. Credit must go to Perry for proving herself in such a different genre, and also to Pink for handling the change of pace and style with aplomb. 'Catch Me While I'm Sleeping' remains one of the very best songs in the Pink catalogue.

If Perry was a risky choice for collaborator on *M!ssundaztood*, now, two years and 12 or more million albums on, picking Rancid's Tim Armstrong made Perry seem like a safe bet. But he acquitted himself well on a series of tracks that borrowed ideas from punk, soul, ska, new wave and electronica to create music that crackled with energy. Armstrong's strong sense of songcraft and pop hooks resulted in songs that grabbed from the off, yet bore repeated listens. All credit to Pink for picking a sidekick who had yet to prove himself in the commercial pop-rock arena.

'Trouble' – which casts Pink as the titular bad girl who you can see coming a mile off, on her way to "disturb my town" – is a strong album opener. Even stronger is 'Last To Know', and if the theme of finding out about a cheating lover is hardly original, the song's hooks are so powerful it feels brand new. 'Tonight's The Night' is R&B-ish, only in the '60s, Stax-ish sense of the word: with its brass and soul strut, it sounds like a cover of an old Wilson Pickett number. 'Oh My God' finds Pink and potty-mouthed rapper Peaches fulfilling their Stevie Nicks and Sapphic fantasies both at once.

The hidden track, 'Hooker' (available only on "explicit" versions of the album – *Try This* was Pink's first album to feature a Parental Advisory warning), is the last Armstrong co-write on the album, and it's an expletive-splattered, vitriolic affair that fingers an unnamed detractor ("You ain't nothin' but a hooker, selling your fuckin' soul") with melodic disdain. 'Save My Life', 'Humble Neighborhoods', 'Walk Away' and 'Unwind' are the sort of AOR the likes of Pat Benatar made her own back in the '80s; their third-person narratives and/or role-playing emphasise the idea that, overall, *Try This* is less consciously confessional, less about Pink, more a series of impromptu jibes and digs at whatever targets Pink had in mind, than its predecessor.

Pink had a problem at the start of the writing and recording of *Try This*: how to repeat the success of *M!ssundaztood* without repeating herself. She was always going to get some criticism, either from fans who didn't want her to stray too far from the formula established on her second album, or from those who wanted her to do what she did after her debut: rip it up and start again. She did a little of both on *Try This*, and so accommodated both camps, although it could be argued that the new targets for her wrath weren't quite as compelling as, say, her dysfunctional family on *M!ssundaztood*'s 'My Vietnam'.

As one reviewer wrote circa the release of *Try This*: "Like it or not, Pink is stuck with the crucial punk dilemma of how to grow up and make maturity matter. Whether she'll squander her rage or rise to the challenge remains to be seen."

Elsewhere, the album received mainly positive reviews from critics with an average rating of 70, indicating generally positive reviews, on the Metacritic website. Of the dissenting voices, *New York Magazine* stated that "Pink pitches a brand of seriousness that is pure Lifetime-TV mawkishness." The *Guardian* newspaper commented that, "Like a lot of pop at the moment, it just sounds like a wan imitation of Pink's second album" while *Entertainment Weekly* gave the album a positive review and called it, "A hooky, engaging throwaway that expands Pink's range while holding on fiercely to her irascible inner child."

In purely commercial terms, *Try This* was not as successful as Pink's second album; indeed, it remains her lowest-selling album to date. It debuted at number nine on the US *Billboard* 200 in November 2003, with first-week sales of 147,000 copies, a weaker debut than that of *M!ssundaztood*. As of May 2, 2004, the album had reached the Top 10 on album charts in the UK, Canada and Australia, where Pink has always been hugely popular. By March 2007, it had sold 719,000 copies in the US and three million copies worldwide, a relative flop compared to its predecessor.

The singles, too, fared less well than previous ones. 'Trouble' and 'God Is a DJ' failed to reach the US Top 40 but went Top 10 in other countries, while 'Last to Know' was only released as a single outside North America (perhaps in recognition of the fact that she was almost more popular outside America, she toured extensively on the Try This Tour through Europe and Australia, where the album was generally better received).

On the upside, 'Trouble' earned Pink her second Grammy Award (for Best Female Rock Vocal Performance), and 'Feel Good Time', which only appeared on non-US versions of the album, was nominated in the category of Best Pop Collaboration with Vocals.

The album's first single, 'Trouble', reached number two in Canada and the Top 10 in the UK and Australia, but it peaked only at number 68 on the US *Billboard* Hot 100 on its release in October 2003. Prior to that, 'Catch Me While I'm Sleeping' had been issued as a promotional single in the US; in the same period, a promo CD-R acetate of 'Humble Neighborhoods' was made available in the UK. Follow-up single 'God Is A DJ' failed to chart on the Hot 100 in March 2004, although it reached number 11 in the UK. A third single, 'Last To Know', was released exclusively in Europe in May 2004 and peaked at 21 in the UK.

Pink embarked on the Try This Tour in Europe during 2004, and a DVD chronicling the tour was released in 2006. Meanwhile, the singles from *Try This* enjoyed a cinematic after-life: 'Trouble' was used in the 2004 film *White Chicks*, the same song was used in *Miss Congeniality 2: Armed And Fabulous*, and 'God Is A DJ' was featured on the soundtrack of the film *Mean Girls*.

As with those from *M!ssundaztood*, Pink and her directors of choice had a field day making the videos for her singles. In the case of 'Trouble' that should read "desert day", because of its Western theme. In the video, Pink rides her horse into a deserted, dusty place called Sharktown. With breasts heaving, our heroine proceeds to beat seven shades of hell out of every man in her path, brawling with customers in the saloon, even the sheriff, who has her locked up in the nearby jail cell. Somehow, she manages to escape, returns to the bar for yet more fighting, and she and several other women – played by none other than the pop girl group the Pussycat Dolls – start dancing on the bar counter.

For 'God Is A DJ', a song about letting go and living life to the fullest, the video storyline involved Pink in skimpy hussy-wear cavorting all over passengers on the subway, and then doing the same to revellers at the local nightclub. Finally, 'Last To Know', her first single in the UK not to hit the Top 20, came with a promotional music video comprising a montage of shots from some of Pink's concerts during her Try This Tour in Europe. A proper video was scheduled to be filmed, but the plan was scrapped after the album sales began to decrease.

Try This might not have been as comprehensive a success as *M!ssundaztood*, but it continued the reinvention of Pink. Even LA Reid, who probably in his heart of hearts still wanted her to be that R&B girl, was cautiously optimistic when he heard the album and its mohawked punk-lite.

"There was never really any conflict," he deadpanned. "I just wanted to make sure she covered her core fan base from the first album. She is a rapidly evolving artist. She can sing like Janis Joplin, she's got the edge and the range. I will be interested to see how *Try This* does. She's found her identity. But we know she can switch it again."

As for Pink, she just had to do what she had to do, and if that meant sacrificing several million sales, so be it. Most of all, it had to be true, honest, real. It had to be Pink.

"I know a lot of people wanted *M!ssundaztood II*," she said on the release of *Try This*. "But I have to go in my own direction. I've grown up. This is me right now. I'm a woman. I'm going through love, insecurity, all those things. I'm also trying to mend relationships with my parents and I'm getting there. With my music, I wear my heart on my sleeve. It's all in there.

"We've all got a journey," she added. "All I know is, I've been down there and I much prefer being up here. I want to keep climbing and I want to keep progressing. It's not a game to me. This is my life."

Chapter 4

Feel Good Time

"I don't want to do anything the way it's been done before, but that's just because real people are rarely allowed to act real in the music business."

Inevitably, given the extent of her success since her debut album, Pink has become almost as well-known for her extracurricular activities as she has for her music. She might not be as notorious as, say, Britney Spears, but that's because her career hasn't followed the same good-girl-gone-bad trajectory: she was bad, or at least "bad-ass", from the start.

Nevertheless, the celebrity of the woman widely credited with making teen-pop go punk has been considerable enough to keep her in the media spotlight even during those lulls when she hasn't had a record to promote – in the period between her third (2003's *Try This*) and fourth (2006's *I'm Not Dead*) albums, for example, she was named one of the 100 Sexiest Artists alive by VH1 and was the recipient of a World

Music award for Best Pop Female Artist. Of course, it hasn't harmed her profile one iota that she's a colourful character who tends not to censor herself or modify her behaviour to suit whatever event at which she happens to be present.

"I like stirring things up and creating dissent and creating discussion and highlighting the ridiculousness of it all – I know I'm a mess of conflicts and flaws!" she has said, cheekily adding: "Funny, isn't it? In the meantime, check the songs I've gotten out of it."

To Pink, doing what she wants at any given moment, with little regard for the consequences, comes as second nature. Take the 2002 MTV Awards, at which she was nominated in the Best Female Video and Best Dance Video categories for 'Get The Party Started', and where she spent much of the ceremony in an advanced state of inebriation. Pink was taken aback at how surprised people were by her antics.

"I just can't believe what people expect of you when you're in the public eye," she told Neil Kulkarni of *Bang* magazine after the event. "They made such a big deal out of me being drunk at the [2002] MTV Awards. Why? People were like, 'You're sending the wrong message.' No, dude. I was bored. I was sitting in that audience, and I didn't think I was ever going to be on camera, because I absolutely didn't think I was gonna win."

According to the singer, she was there with her friends, just "hanging out and having fun – we like to party and have a good time". Her production manager was being helpful, making sure everyone's glass was full: "He kept bringing me beers," she said, "so of course I'm gonna drink." Eventually, by the time her name got called, she was pretty much gone.

"I was in shock," she recalled. "I got up there [on the stage] and everybody was looking at me and all of a sudden I felt like, y'know, where you have that dream when you go to school and you realise you don't have any clothes on and everyone's looking at you... and that's how I felt for the first time in my life. And I was like, 'I am too drunk for this. I've nothing to say to any of you. Thanks...'"

As Pink explained, her strategy at all times is to not do what's expected of her: "You act normal and people think you're a freak. I don't want to do anything the way it's been done before, but that's just because real people are rarely allowed to act real in the music business."

She cited as an example of her unconventional pop star behaviour her refusal to use bodyguards while out and about, something that has gotten her into hot bother on more than one occasion, such as the time she was walking around New York alone. "A woman tried to kidnap me in Times Square," she told the *Mail On Sunday*. "It was actually very funny. I was just walking around, doing my thing, and this woman came up to me and said, 'Hey, you're Pink.' I just nodded and smiled and then she grabbed me by the arm and said, 'I'm taking you to my aunt's house.'" A lot of celebrities, explained Pink, have problems with public confrontations. Not this one. "It doesn't worry me at all," she said. "I can handle myself. I know my martial arts. I looked at her [the woman in Times Square] and said, 'I don't think so.' She wouldn't let go and was trying to drag me towards the subway. There was a little bit of me that was sort of laughing inside, thinking, 'Am I the only person this sort of thing happens to?' In the end I just shook her firmly and shouted 'No' really loud." Pink almost regretted her decision. "When she'd gone I thought I should have asked her if her aunt made a good spaghetti Bolognese. If she'd said yes, I would have gone."

Another example of her obduracy was her refusal up to that

point to write a conventional love song. Even 'Love Song', the last track on *Try This*, was about not being in love. "I never wrote love songs before that album, and I couldn't just do some 'I love you' song where I'm singing to some guy eye-to-eye," she said. "Love isn't like that. I want to write love songs that are about the fear that love gives you. I can't settle for anything too obvious."

It's debatable whether anyone expected the outrageous, gregarious, tattooed wild girl with the Day-Glo pink hair to openly flirt or even kiss women in public, but that's exactly what she did as soon as she achieved worldwide fame and the media's gaze was trained on her. Besides, according to Pink, the assumption was always that she swung both ways anyway.

"I'm proud that people think I'm gay," she told journalist Louise Gannon. "Everyone has always thought I was gay because of the tattoos, the short hair, the attitude. But I don't care. I love to challenge people's preconceptions. Loads of my friends are lesbians and it really annoys me that gay people aren't allowed to get married in most parts of America. I'd go on a march for gay rights any time."

In October 2003, Pink flaunted her lack of concern for how she may be perceived, sexually, when she was photographed getting up close and personal with actress Kristanna Loken, who had just starred in *Terminator 3: Rise Of The Machines*, even though the singer had already been linked with professional motocross racer Carey Hart since the 2001 X Games in Philadelphia, as well as with Rancid rocker Lars Frederiksen. She and Loken were, in fact, seen together on more than one occasion: the papers reported that "the stunning pair – the leggy blonde and the 'Get The Party Started' rock chick – were snapped sharing lusty kisses at a party in Monte Carlo on Saturday night, and the next night they continued their antics at exclusive nightclub Jimmy'z." As they "got cosy" on the dancefloor and "shared an intimate moment as they gazed into each other's eyes", a fellow clubber exclaimed, "They barely came up for air. They were rubbing against each other and hands were everywhere." Apparently on the night in question Pink went ballistic when she spotted a photographer and dragged Loken into a dark corner for a bit of privacy, but it wasn't long before they were in full view of everyone again. Loken told the press: "Kissing a girl is much, much nicer than kissing a man. I think it is more intimate to be honest. I suppose it is more sensitive. I think females bond better than with men, although I do find men attractive. Sometimes girls just want to go for it with a female friend. And usually you'll get a good reaction from men who are looking at you. It wasn't the first time I kissed a girl when I kissed Pink, you know – oh God, no. But I won't give too much away."

That November, Pink caused a mild stir when she appeared at the American Music Awards, where she performed an acoustic version of her hit 'Trouble', sporting a new vintage Hollywood-style blonde and black hairstyle. She had already thrilled fans on the red carpet before the show, by arriving in a see-through black dress, which showed off some racy, lacy lingerie, although she was almost upstaged by her nemesis Britney Spears who ripped off a long silver coat to reveal a daring pink and black leather outfit, a figure-hugging pink and black corset, skimpy black pants and thigh-length chaps as she opened the ceremony at Los Angeles' Shrine Auditorium. And R&B star Ashanti was another artist vying for the media's attention as she performed her hit 'Rain On Me' – in an actual indoor rain shower! – wearing only a flimsy pink mini dress. Meanwhile, teenage singer-actress Hilary Duff also showed off a new look – adding Christina Aguilera-style black streaks to her blonde hair for her performance of 'So Yesterday', ditching her good-girl image to rock out in high-heeled leather boots and an all-black number.

In December 2003, Pink became part of another celebrity "hot couple", albeit a heterosexual one this time, when she was seen out and about with Mötley Crüe drummer – and, notoriously, erstwhile other half of Pamela Anderson – Tommy Lee. According to a report in one of America's scandal sheets, he and Pink were "so desperate to get their hands on each other" at a party that they "indulged in some raunchy antics in a toilet." Wrote a passing journalist: "The wild twosome – who began dating last month – were spotted getting steamed up in New York nightspot Lotus by promoter Ronnie Madras, who was quite taken aback by what he saw." The promoter recounted that "Tommy and Pink had already caused raised eyebrows by taking it in turns to make out with a mystery woman in their banquette before disappearing to the bathroom," adding that, when he stumbled in on them, "Tommy was allegedly simulating sex with the 'Trouble' singer in front of a urinal."

Whether or not Pink was attempting to increase interest in her third album *Try This*, which had met with initially disappointing sales on its release in November 2003, is arguable, although her antics did manage to keep her in the public eye. With regard to her relationship with rock monster Tommy Lee, she said, predictably, that they were "just good friends", adding that he was "a fun guy with a bad rep".

"He's awesome," she exclaimed. "We met at a party and we just clicked as friends. He's fun to hang out with. He doesn't give a shit, which is rare."

As for she and Kristanna Loken, she teased a reporter: "Whatever you saw, it all happened." Was she, asked the scribe, a friend of hers? "She was that night," replied Pink, referring to the evening when they locked lips. "We just danced and she kissed me. She tried to dominate me, although I won't be dominated."

Pink then addressed the question of her sexuality, and why people seemed keen to label her as a lesbian icon, or even a lesbian. Why did she think that was?

"I don't know. I guess cos I'm tough," she laughed. "A lot of my friends are gay, most of my girlfriends are. I don't mind at all. When I started, it was, 'Is she white, is she black, is she mixed, is she Hispanic?' Actually, I'm Irish-German-Lithuanian-Jew... But right now it's, 'Is she gay, is she straight, is she bi... is she tri? What is she?'"

Did Pink think that it would be easier to have a relationship with a woman? "Fuck, no!" she replied. "Women like to talk about everything, way too much shit... If I was with a woman I'd be the guy in the relationship. Like, 'Come on, shut up!'"

Pink, who has described herself as "trisexual" because she'll "try anything once", has said of men that "they're just as sensitive and insecure as women. I can't tell you how many of my male friends take longer to get ready than me – it's crazy! It just goes to show that we all have our hang-ups, and I find that reassuring." She admitted that only once did a man ever try to change her, but she told him where to get off.

"I once dated a man," she told *Cosmopolitan*, "who said he wanted me to be more ladylike. I told him where to stick it! Independence is what makes you special. A lot of people change in relationships. It's as though they mould into the other person's ideal. But you lose a big part of yourself and part of the person he fell in love with in the first place. No woman should change to suit a man." The *Cosmo* journalist wondered whether Pink's strong, independent persona intimidated men.

"Not the men I know," she said. "I think there's something hugely attractive about people who know their own mind."

Was she really as tough as she seemed, or was it an act? "It's not an act," she told *Look* magazine, revealing that she regularly cries during puppy food commercials. "People just choose to see that side of me. I'm very kind. The toughest people are the most sensitive. We have to create this shell, as if we're saying, 'I'll push you away; you can't hurt me.'"

Pink spoke about her Sapphic tendencies in an interview with Craig McLean for the *Independent On Sunday*. She told him about her formative childhood experiences. "I was never a lesbian but I've had my moments," she admitted. "I had a girl-friend when I was 13 and she left me for my brother! That kind of fucked me up. We held hands and we kissed and that was my girlfriend, that's what you do when you're 13! And she left me for my fucking brother, which was bizarre and twisted and fucked-up and gross. My brother used to steal all my girl-friends... But I think women are beautiful, and most of my friends are gay. I love women, especially curvy ones. We are the sexiest things. When you see a nice, curvy woman you think, well, why not?"

Inevitably, Pink was interviewed by gay bible *Attitude*. In the magazine article, she spoke enthusiastically about her "leg-endary" gig at London nightclub G-A-Y: "I had so much fun. The audience was amazing. It was so wild. Every city every-where I go it's a mixed gay and straight audience, but that was a really fun energy. I would say that was one of my favourite shows I've ever done." She also fielded questions about her sexuality from the readers of *Attitude*, particularly one wonder-ing whether she was, in fact, a lesbian. She responded: "I want to make that person happy but I can't right now. I have dabbled but right now I'm strictly 'dickly'. What do I find sexy in a girl?

I'm not really sure. It's all about energy and confidence – whether it's a girl or a boy." Another reader enquired about her "strong connection" with the gay community "from day one" and mused that it was Pink's androgynous image, and her brash forthright attitude, that so endeared her to gay fans.

"I guess I was aware of it on my first tour," she said. "I guess I am kind of androgynous and I love that; it's why I love Annie Lennox. For me, most of my friends are gay. Actually, I won't say most but a lot. And before that most of my friends were black. I think I identify with people who have had some sort of struggle along the way. I wouldn't say I was a fag hag. I'm more of a 'cluster fuck' – meaning I bring all different kinds of people together, and I love that."

On a less positive note, in January 2004 Pink was involved in a contretemps with Britney Spears and Beyoncé Knowles, her two co-stars in a new Pepsi TV advert that saw the three global megastars playing scantily clad gladiators in a scene out of Ancient Rome, in an amphitheatre surrounded by baying hordes and an emperor played by Enrique Iglesias. Apparently, Britney stunned her female co-stars when she stormed out on them, following a "bitter row" with the Destiny's Child beauty during filming of the soft drinks promo. The three stood united during the premiere of the advert in London, but later launched into "a heated confrontation" at the capital's Nobu restaurant, according to Britain's *Daily Star* tabloid. Although event organisers had reportedly tried to keep the warring threesome apart, the singers sat down for dinner together at the plush restaurant – until Spears ran out just 10 minutes into the meal. One of those ever-reliable "sources close to the stars" said, "It was ridiculous. Pepsi fork out millions to get this super-trio together for an advert and they can't even be civil to each other for the duration of a meal. Beyoncé was sniping at

Britney who was giving as good as she got. Pink stonewalled the pair of them. It looked like it was going to turn nasty, then Britney stormed out with a face like thunder."

The following month, Pink was in the news again, only this time there was nothing particularly controversial about it; it was just actress Drew Barrymore thrilling viewers of US TV comedy show *Saturday Night Live* with rowdy impersonations of Pink as well as of actress Charlize Theron, of America's former first lady Hillary Rodham Clinton as she might have been back in the '60s, of ill-fated octogenarian-fancier Anna Nicole Smith and of troubled rocker Courtney Love.

Later that year, rumours began to spread that Pink was due to play the lead role in a movie biopic of the late, legendary wild woman of rock, Janis Joplin. Oddly, Renée Zellweger had also been lined up to star in another, completely separate but identical film about the '60s rocker, who died of a heroin and alcohol overdose in a Hollywood hotel room in October 1970 at the age of 27. The rival Zellweger vehicle, tentatively titled *Piece Of My Heart* after the Joplin song, had been shelved due to producers not being able to decide on a script, leaving the way clear for Pink's version of events, provisionally titled *The Gospel According To Janis*. If it happened, it would be a lifetime's ambition realised for Pink, who had adored Joplin for years, for her music and for her no-nonsense, take-no-prisoners attitude.

It was Joplin, more than anyone, who taught Pink that she didn't have to be a regular cutesy half-naked girly-girl to succeed as a pop-rock star. In fact, she once claimed that the only artist who she ever really wanted to be like was Joplin, which might explain the bluesy rasp in her voice and the fearless, ballsy way she comports herself.

"Janis Joplin is my mentor in life, way more than musically, just spiritually," she said. "She was the original rebel: she kept her clothes on and she made more of a difference than most people."

There was some confusion about Pink's cinematic future in December 2004 when it was announced that she would be exposing her innermost thoughts and feelings and recounting the story of her rise to global stardom in a film based on her personal diaries. This was following the decision to postpone the mooted Joplin biopic. Pink, whose acting experience thus far had been limited to a cameo role in *Charlie's Angels: Full Throttle*, said, "I plan to write a film script based on them [my diaries]. They are shocking, inspiring and, above all, true to my heart." She added that she intended to call the movie, with admirable concision, *The Diary Of Pink*.

The following April, Pink was back in the news by proxy when it was reported that her on-off biker boyfriend Corey Hart would be among the stars of the fifth series of bizarre US celebrity reality show *The Surreal Life*, in which a group of celebrities were taped 24 hours a day while living together in a Hollywood Hills mansion. He would be appearing alongside British model Caprice, Sylvester Stallone's ex Janice Dickinson, shamed former baseball player José Canseco, Salt-N-Pepa star Sandi Denton, actor Bronson Pinchot and reality TV diva Omerosa Manigault-Stallworth. Later that year, Pink collaborated with her good friend Lisa Marie Presley on the track 'Shine', on Presley's sophomore album *Now What*.

By 2006, the Joplin project was once again on the agenda. Almost two years after it was first mooted, with Pink in the starring role, it had now become something of a celeb cat-fight, with actress Zooey Deschanel now the favourite to play the tragic rock icon, beating Lindsay Lohan, Britney Spears, Scarlett Johansson – and Pink herself – to the coveted role.

Pink had originally been director Penelope Spheeris' first choice to play the late rocker, but she pulled out, blaming the movie's producers for turning the casting process into "some circus pop contest – who's the 'it' girl who wants to play Janis." It was reported that *Almost Famous* beauty Deschanel, 26, had signed to play Joplin in *The Gospel According To Janis*, which was to start filming in Philadelphia, Pennsylvania, in November 2006. The film was scheduled for release in 2008. Oscar winner Renée Zellweger's own film about Joplin's life, *Piece Of My Heart*, was now on hold at Paramount Pictures while the script was reworked.

Meanwhile, Deschanel had spent four months working with a vocal coach to help her mimic Joplin's gritty vocals, as she was due to sing all of Joplin's songs featured in the film. According to producer Peter Newman, it had been a struggle to find an actress who could sing or a singer who could act. He said, "Zooey is the first we found who excels at both."

With Pink literally out of the picture, it was probably time for her to do what she did best and reacquaint herself with her fans – fans of her music. After all, she hadn't released a new album in two and a half years, and two and a half years is a lifetime in pop. In fact, as far as pop audiences were concerned, with Pink out of the charts since early 2004, she may as well have been dead. How typical of the singer, then, to announce that the title of her forthcoming fourth album would indeed be *I'm Not Dead*.

Chapter 5

Trouble

"What has surprised me most is that a lot of people agree with the point but hate that it's coming from me. I've been called a hypocrite. Some people have been offended by it, but that's cool. I like to push those buttons. I like dissent in the ranks."

Pink has long since proved that she's no fool: she is, officially, 'Not Stupid'. But part of her appeal, her shtick if you like, is the way that she assumes a position away from her pop-girl peers, to emphasise her apartness from the others. In February 2006, she offered her most explicit statement of difference when she unveiled her first new record since May 2004's 'Last To Know', the single 'Stupid Girls', one of her most contentious releases to date.

Written by Pink in conjunction with Billy Mann, Niklas Olovson and Robin Mortensen Lynch, it was the first release from Pink's fourth album, *I'm Not Dead*. It was her biggest US hit since 2002 and earned her a nomination for Best Female

Pop Vocal Performance at the 2007 Grammy Awards. The single entered the US *Billboard* Hot 100 chart at number 24 at the end of February, that week's highest new entry and the highest debuting single of Pink's career (although it was later topped by her 2008 single, 'So What'). A week after release, it climbed to number 13, becoming Pink's eighth Top 20 hit in the States and her highest-peaking single since 'Just Like A Pill' in 2002. It was finally certified gold by the RIAA two years later, in February 2008.

It was a bigger hit elsewhere – it reached the Top 10 in most countries in Europe, number two on the Canadian Singles Chart, and on the Australian ARIA Singles Chart it entered at number four and was certified gold for sales of over 35,000. It also peaked at number four on the UK Singles Chart, becoming Pink's highest-charting single in Britain since 'Feel Good Time' in 2003. Meanwhile, the music video that accompanied the single, in which Pink parodied celebrities such as Lindsay Lohan, Jessica Simpson, Mary-Kate Olsen and Paris Hilton, won the MTV Video Music Award for Best Pop Video in August 2006. When she received the award, Pink mimicked Paris Hilton, one of the 'Stupid Girls' she was supposedly critiquing in the single, by talking in a high-pitched voice and acting in a gushing, over-excited manner. Nicole Richie, Hilton's co-star on reality show *The Simple Life*, co-presented the award.

Pink was apparently inspired to write 'Stupid Girls' as the Size Zero debate began to rage amid fears that hyper-sexualised, airheaded celebs were proving irresistible icons for legions of suggestible teenagers. She called it "the antidote-anthem for everything I had been thinking about women and thinness." In the song she expresses her dismay at the dearth of positive role models for young women while encouraging them to aim higher, after she noticed the silly little rich girls and scantily clad bimbos – the wannabe Paris Hiltons and Lindsay Lohans – near her Los Angeles home. "There's a certain thing the world is being fed, and my point is there should be a choice," Pink said, adding that the song was "brought on by several conversations I've had with women and girls. Women have fought so long and hard for our rights and equality, and now all our attention is put on being a Size Zero."

Some girls, she went on, are "living vicariously through these people who seem to shop all day" rather than focusing on issues such as war and poverty. In the song, Pink rails against the "paparazzi girls" with their "itsy-bitsy doggies", their "teeny-weeny tees" and push-up bras, alluding to the glamour models and heiresses who obsess over designer handbags, fake tans and cosmetic surgery; the video took to task the skeletal, orange-skinned doyennes of the tabloids and gossip mags. One scene in particular was disturbing: the one in the club toilet where a starlet pushes a toothbrush down her throat to make herself sick.

Even the International Association of Eating Disorder Professionals weighed into the debate, determining that the song "highlights the culture's relentless and unrealistic pursuit of thinness and unattainable drive for physical beauty". It's not often that you get a professional medical body issuing press statements supporting the lyrics of a song and the use of the visual imagery in the accompanying video. But the IAEDP said this of 'Stupid Girls' and its allusions to bulimia: "This is an opportunity to remind people about the seriousness of eating disorders, which have devastating effects as individuals struggle to achieve social acceptance and self-worth. Furthermore, the video highlights how life-consuming an eating disorder can be. We are hoping that women can see the unglamorous side of celebrity popularity founded on physical beauty alone. The IAEDP does not intend to endorse Pink's personal position but at the same time we applaud a recording artist who states that if women waste their time, money and energy on trying to be someone else's idea of 'fabulous', they waste their potential to be something better."

Pink discussed what she called the "Stupid Girl epidemic" during an appearance on *The Oprah Winfrey Show*, while the song was praised by none other than Harry Potter author J. K. Rowling on her official website.

Unusually, it was decided to release the video one month before issuing the song to radio, a wise gambit as it turned out: 8.6 million people downloaded the video when it was made available on the Internet. As for radio programmers, eager to air it for listeners, they went online to download the audio from the video in order to broadcast it ahead of its official release.

The video was directed by Dave Meyers, responsible for clips for everyone from Dido to Slipknot. Pink described it as "sick and twisted and insane" and said of Meyers, "He has an insane imagination. I don't think anyone ever stopped laughing during [the making of] 'Stupid Girls'. I don't think everyone else is going to laugh, but just know that we all did."

The video, for which she did her own stunts, shows Pink as both angel and demon trying to influence the future of a young girl. The angel shows her a series of images demonstrating the vapidity of current trends in female celebrity, and the scenes feature Pink in various roles, including a dancer in a rap video to correspond with the lyric about dreaming of a girl president dancing in a video with 50 Cent; a girl attempting to attract the attention of an instructor at the gym; a girl who inflates her blow-up breasts at a bowling alley; a girl at a tanning salon; a girl with a purging disorder who considers calories "so not sexy"; an old woman in a pink tracksuit; a girl getting plastic surgery; a girl making a sex tape; a girl provocatively washing her car and rubbing a face-cloth and soap all over herself; and a girl who goes into what looks like a pet shop, buys an "itsy-bitsy doggy", and drives her car so distractedly while applying her makeup that she runs over two pedestrians. Pink also plays characters designed to represent the polar opposite of the titular dumb females, such as a finishing school teacher, a female President and a girl winning a game of football. The video ends with the girl choosing a football, a computer, books, dance shoes and a keyboard over makeup and a set of dolls: the demon is defeated.

Some of the negatively portrayed characters in the video are parodies of young female celebrities such as the ultra-skinny Mary Kate Olsen – the girl who visits the Fred Segal clothing store in the video is dressed in Olsen's trademark boho-chic style. The redheaded girl who accidentally mows down passers-by with her car is meant to be Lindsay Lohan. The scene in which Pink washes a car in a bikini is a parody of similar scenes in the video for Jessica Simpson's 2005 single 'These Boots Are Made For Walkin''. And the grainy, black and white digital video images showing Pink in bed with a man are visual quotes from the infamous Paris Hilton sex tape *1 Night In Paris*.

For a three-and-a-half-minute clip, it made quite an impact, and attracted plenty of attention, with appraisals both positive and negative. Some considered Pink's position to be somewhat hypocritical considering she had herself been sold partly on her looks. "'Stupid Girls' tries to recapture the mission-statement feeling of *M!ssundaztood* but fails owing to a lack of generosity," wrote one hostile reviewer. "The song and the video seek to distinguish Pink from Lindsay, Paris, and Jessica, and the lyrics sincerely ask, 'Where, oh where, have the smart people gone?' Pink has shown no small amount of flesh in her rise to the top, so calling out anyone else's bra tactics is a highly suspect move. She's no stranger to the Hilton Doctrine ('I'll do what I want, cuz I can'). And 'smart' isn't really Pink's stock-in-trade. She's a female version of Aerosmith's Steven Tyler, a skilled ham, long on humour and vigour, but hardly a visionary."

Others saw it as a deliberate attempt to court controversy as part of a broader effort to rescue her career following the relative failure of the *Try This* album. Then again, Pink used to hump a blow-up Christina Aguilera doll onstage (one night it burst), and perform ironic lap-dances for audience members. She had never been afraid to use her sexuality. "I'm a very sexual being," she has said. "I don't think there's anything wrong with being, acting, dressing or talking sexy if you're doing it for your own pleasure. And not just giving it away." She admitted that she, too, had fantasies of being super-thin, but she was not, she said, prepared to do anything dangerous to achieve it. "I'd love to be thinner," she said, "but I don't have the discipline to be anorexic or bulimic. And I'm not willing to hurt myself to do it. I'd rather be strong than skinny, nourished than starving."

She was also, she laughed, too much of a fan of fried foods, not to mention other such unhealthy fare as booze and fags, to become abstemious for the sake of her appearance. Would she subject herself to plastic surgery? "I would like to have children, and if I have my 13 kids, and my boobs are down here," she said, pointing to the floor, "then I'm going to have to bring them back up. But I'm such a hypochondriac, I would get freaked out if I didn't know how my nose was ageing. And I find women who are on the beach, with a cigarette hanging out of their mouth, topless, tits sagging, Martini in their hand, just gorgeous. I want to be able to see how many times I've laughed in my life."

She concluded: "I don't even think these girls are stupid, it's just an act: be a Size Zero, have a certain handbag, don't contribute to the world, just shop, don't think. [But] there's not enough examples of how cool it is to be smart and healthy and not make yourself sick trying to attain society's ideal of beautiful. It's about an entire generation, a culture and mentality, that I just find so boring. And I find it frustrating that I have to Google and search for smart responsible women – women I never get to see on the cover of a magazine unless they're getting a divorce or a boob job or having a great pair of shoes or going to a cool party."

In an interview with Spanish TV Pink listed some non-'Stupid Girls' of whom she was a fan: Alicia Keys, Fiona Apple, Björk, Norah Jones, Joss Stone. She told the Spanish interviewer that 'Stupid Girls' was the first song that she wrote for her new album; before putting pen to paper, she feared that she had run out of ideas. "When I started this album I had nothing to say, and I thought I sucked!" she said. "Then I wrote 40 songs..." 'Stupid Girls', she declared, was "a wake-up call to the new generation of girls. They used to want to change the world, now they just care about handbags and lipstick and how good they look. Well, don't lump me in with that category. Some of us are active and do want to change the world."

Intriguingly, according to one source, 'Stupid Girls' was "explicitly inspired" by Ariel Levy's book *Female Chauvinist Pigs: Women And The Rise Of Raunch Culture*. In the book, the author wonders why women today are embracing those aspects of the culture, particularly highly sexualised young girls, that would have caused their feminist foremothers to throw up their arms in despair. Levy explores the intertwined

concepts of modern feminism and sexual liberation, the impli-
cations of each and what it really means to be "empowered".

"I think the main thing here is that an awful lot of people
are relieved that someone's actually talking about these things
in public," said Pink, who admitted that she hadn't heard
directly from the girls she lampooned in the song, but that her
people did have to field a couple of calls from said celebs' pub-
licists. She did admit, though, that Paris Hilton, for one, had
revealed to Pink her distress at her portrayal in the video. She
issued a statement in which she implied that she was using it to
launch her comeback. "She said that?" asked an aggrieved
Pink. "Well, spell it, Paris. Spell comeback." Hilton was still
miffed years later, and approached Pink in a nightclub to say: "I
hope you realise that the person I seem to be in the press is
really just an act and the real me is really smart." Pink replied:
"Just get over it. The song was, like, years ago. Quit bugging
me." She did, however, add that, "There's part of me that thinks
they're such losers, but there's also a part of me that admires
how they actually play the game. I'm so bad at playing the
Hollywood game. I just hate all that fake stuff."

Pink, who once declared that "the coolest thing is to piss the
most people off", went on: "What has surprised me most is
that a lot of people agree with the point but hate that it's coming from me. I've been called a hypocrite. Then again, I've also
been called fat. Some people have been offended by it, but
that's cool. I like to push those buttons. I like dissent in the
ranks. I think it was important that I got a letter from the eating disorders body congratulating me on what I said and what
I showed. These diseases – and they are diseases – are very, very
unhealthy. The video started off being humorous, but the point
is there that you don't have to kill yourself to meet society's
ideal for beauty."

Pink's contention, one espoused by the IAEDP, was that a whole generation of young women were starving themselves, causing serious damage to their menstrual cycle and normal metabolic rate just to win male attention. She also felt they were acting stupid to make themselves seem more adorable.

"These girls have dumbed themselves down to appear cute. How bad is that?" she wondered. "I feel that it's just the one image of women out there which is being fed to society. There needs to be more alternatives, options and examples about how you can be cool without the silly handbag and without acting like a bimbo. I can't get my head around this: it is lucrative to dumb yourself down. I cannot believe that the smarter version of the truth is not more interesting. I refuse to be stupid to get somewhere or get something."

She said she was doing her bit for "tolerance for diversity in the world" and that she was using humour to address the problems of bulimia and anorexia. "Eating disorders are diseases and they're very, very serious. And scary, and rampant! And I make fun of it – but really, I'm making fun of the idea that a girl feels like she needs to do that in order to be important. And I have the same issues. That's why I can write about this stuff. That's why I have to make it ridiculous – because I have to get over it myself as well." She revealed that she had self-worth issues, too. "Always! You can't be a girl and not have some sort of issue with yourself. I think it's genetic. You see people like Oprah [Winfrey], a lot of different women who have these struggles, but they're so important and so smart that you think, why the hell would you worry about that? And women in Africa who don't have time to worry about how they look because there are more important problems."

Ironically, Pink's record label hadn't even wanted to release

'Stupid Girls' as the first single from her fourth album, and there were heated debates about the subject. Initially, LA Reid et al wanted her to work on a single with Max Martin, the Swedish one-man hit factory who penned songs for Britney Spears among others and wrote the song 'U + Ur Hand' for *I'm Not Dead*, which the label loved and earmarked as the first release, keen for a safe bet as the first single. Pink got her own way in the end, although it's not known how happy her people were with the ensuing controversy and media firestorm.

This was not the first time Pink had done something controversial – nor would it be the last. This was, after all, the young woman who, as a spokesperson for PETA (People for the Ethical Treatment of Animals), fired off an angry missive to Britain's royal family after Prince William invited her to perform as the musical guest of honour at his 21st birthday party. She wrote back saying that she couldn't until he'd explained why he went hunting. The letter read: "I was happy to learn that I was your first choice to play at your 21st birthday bash, then disgusted to learn that you hunt and kill animals for fun. I hope you learn to change your ways. I did. I used to wear fur until I became a supporter of PETA. Call me or PETA if you'd like any suggestions as to how you should treat animals. Then maybe I'll come and play at your next birthday." The young Prince never replied, which Pink publicly declared "a bit rude". "I want to make people think about their responsibilities," she said. "I don't care if they have a crown."

Later, in advance of an appearance at the Prince's Trust concert, she wrote another letter, this time to the Queen herself, asking why the bearskins of the Buckingham Palace guards couldn't be synthetic, although from some quarters there were accusations of hypocrisy levelled at Pink, a vegetarian who nevertheless wears leather. "I suggested cheaper, more humane alternatives [to HRH]," she said. "Stella McCartney was ready with a design. But I didn't get a reply. How did I address her? I think I wrote, 'To whom it may concern.' Not, 'Dear The Queen.'" In November 2006, Pink even announced her disgust at one of America's pop royalty, Beyoncé, for choosing to wear fur. You can just imagine how Pink would have expressed her disdain for King of Rap Jay-Z's other half: stupid girl.

'Stupid Girls' wasn't the only track from *I'm Not Dead* to create a furore in the press. The song 'Dear Mr. President', written in the form of an open letter, was a scathing attack on America's former commander-in-chief, and it was all the more startling considering it came from someone from the normally anodyne world of mainstream pop.

The song was relentless in its assault, and it was given extra poignancy and potency by being an acoustic number, allowing more space for Pink's angry vocal to be heard. It denounced, among other things, Bush's stance on abortion and his failure to help the homeless during his occupancy of the White House by putting a series of uncomfortable questions to this most unpopular of presidents: how did he feel about the homeless, who did he pray for, who did he see in the mirror, was he proud of what he'd done, how did he sleep and, finally, even though her own older brother Jason was in the military, did he dream about mothers who had no chance to say goodbye to her sons. She later explained: "I support the soldiers. Freedom is something to fight for, but only if that's what you're really fighting for. My dad, Jim, is a Vietnam veteran and is my all-time hero. I get more and more like him. He was the one who taught me to question everything. I question the people in power. Bush is an idiot. The sooner he's gone, the better."

On 'Dear Mr President' Pink went on to attack Dubya's stance on abortion and his decision not to legalise gay marriages with a series of further questions, asking what kind of father would take away his daughter's rights whether that same father would hate her if she was gay. Finally, Pink turns her attention to labour and the minimum wage, declaiming Bush's attitude towards poverty, especially for single mothers.

Recorded with folky American duo, and proud lesbians, the Indigo Girls, this was probably the most outspoken song about a current President ever recorded by a supposedly teen-pop artist, with lyrics that might be considered libellous if printed in a newspaper, especially the allusions to Bush's (erstwhile) penchant for whiskey and cocaine. When she finished recording the track, Pink joked, "Now I'm going to be audited every year. But it was worth it."

Pink had never sounded so engaged and enraged, the result, she said, of her insistence on living in the real world. "I don't hang out with celebrities," she said. "I hang out with real, nine-to-five people. My family are working-class people. I'm very much in tune with what's going on. I don't sit holed up inside my mansion with my poodles and think that everything's fine. I have people that are in Sri Lanka, in Iraq, in Africa working with the UN. I have women in Philadelphia, friends that are poor, who are single parents."

She admitted that she felt an obligation, a sense of duty, to be political – because if not her, then who? "People are so afraid to say things," she said. "When I write songs like 'Dear Mr. President', nothing matters except that I'm doing what I want to do." She explained that, for a while, she had become increasingly incensed by the Bush administration. "The last few years,

I've been reading *The New York Times* and watching the news, and I've been pissed off; I was nauseated by what I saw." However, she also said: "It's a song that could have been written for any President – it's more about the state of the world than any one person. I could have asked these questions to the last President and the President before that.

"It's provocative and questioning," she said, "not flag-waving and 'burn in hell.'" She described it as "the hardest song I've ever written", especially considering she was a "quote/ unquote pop star who's not supposed to say anything or contribute anything." Was she worried about the repercussions, or concerned that it would affect her career in the US? "No," she said, "I wasn't concerned at all. I was angry and I needed to write that open letter. There weren't really any repercussions. I got booed on stage once, which I thought was hilarious. I was opening up for Justin Timberlake in Anaheim, California, and I got booed. I really, really enjoyed it. To create dissent: that's what democracy is. I was just exercising my right."

Chapter 6

Cuz She Can

"I feel like there's a hole and I know how to fill it. People aren't talking trash anymore. I was just feeling really creative and really emotionally available again, and it came out great."

Pink's fourth long-player, released in April 2006, was originally going to be called *Long Way To Happy*, after a song on the album, but Pink changed her mind because she thought *I'm Not Dead* made for a stronger statement of intent; the intention being to announce to the world that, after three years off the pop-rock circuit, she still had plenty to say and plenty of energy with which to say it.

The album was aptly named, because she couldn't have sounded less moribund, more vital, fresh and bursting with angry energy. She knew it, too. "It's about being alive and feisty and not sitting down and shutting up even though people would like you to," she said of the title, which she added came from "an awakening" after her dad had a heart attack. It was about how "it felt good to feel again".

"I turned 25, I started reading the *New York Times*. I started caring less about my drama and more about the world around me," she claimed. "I just kind of woke up and realised I have so much to learn, whereas before I thought I knew everything. That's definitely a huge part of that title."

According to Pink, she did not expect to be very emotionally involved in the making of the album because the experience of making her last, *Try This*, was so "draining", an assertion that contradicts somewhat her statements of the time. In an interview given around the release of 2003's *Try This*, she said of her two weeks spent writing songs in the back of Tim Armstrong and Rancid's tour bus, "It was one of the raddest times. I felt honoured." She seemed to thoroughly enjoy her stint with the US punks, even – especially – when they were misbehaving. Did they clean up their act at all when she was around? "Fuck, no," she said, "but Tim's very much a gentleman. They're clean and sober, so it's, like, have fun, hang out, then work."

Nevertheless, the implication, at least in retrospect, was that she wasn't quite as involved in the process of writing and recording *Try This* as it appeared at the time. For *I'm Not Dead*, she explained, she was "forced to be almost emotionally involved" by her latest co-writers and producers such as Billy Mann, Max Martin (who wrote Britney Spears' '…Baby One More Time'), Josh Abraham, Luke Gottwald, Butch Walker and Mike Elizondo, a far more pop-oriented bunch than her collaborators on *Try This*. "I guess I was just kind of at that place where I felt like I had something to add to the world," she said. "I feel like there's a hole and I know how to fill it. People aren't talking trash anymore. I was just feeling really creative and really emotionally available again, and it came out great."

In the build-up to the album, she did indeed enjoy a creative spurt, penning more than 40 songs. The subject matter? "Everything," she said, "that I could possibly think of." The tracks – on which Pink got credit on the sleeve as producer, as well as for vocals, backing vocals, keyboard and piano – ranged across the spectrum from the personal to the political and back again. The opening track, 'Stupid Girls', was an aural assault that listeners might have found either exhilarating or infuriating; as detailed in the last chapter, it was Pink's critique of a generation of females who she regarded as lacking in proper ambition. Second track, the plaintive 'Who Knew', which would be the second track lifted from the album for single release (after 'Stupid Girls'), addressed "the death of friendship". "You're best friends forever, and then three years later you haven't seen each other in two years – what happened?" she asked rhetorically. "You grow apart and people come in and out of your life for different reasons, seasons." On another level, it was literally about the death of friends, several of whom had died as a result of drug overdoses when she was young. According to Pink, the song was about more than one person: "There's a couple of different people mixed in... It's just the grieving process. You can look at somebody, he might be right there, and the next Monday he might not be." In an interview with the television station TV3 she said that she "always wanted to write a song about death because I came in contact with death at a very young age."

Elsewhere, she was quick to point out the savage irony that it could so easily have been her on the mortuary slab, and that even the deaths of loved ones hadn't put her off drugs when she was a hell-raising teen. "No, they didn't, because I was so young," she explained. "You don't think about mortality, you have nothing to lose at that point." Why did she believe that people were unable to resist Class A narcotics? "A lot of it is just boredom, being lost, not knowing what you're good at." She acknowledged the risk of writing about her drug-abusing past, and that, no matter how critical she was of it, some fans might have felt encouraged to try it out for themselves. "I don't regret where I've come from, and I'm especially proud of the fact I'm not there anymore. But young people are out there listening, and they think, 'She did that, so I can, too.'"

The third song, 'Long Way To Happy', used blistering hard rock and a coruscating vocal from Pink to tell a terrible tale of teenage rape; it was based on jottings on the theme of sexual abuse that Pink made when she was a teen herself. "It's a poem I started when I was 13 and I finally finished it. It's about abuse and it's a common thing," she said, adding, "I know a lot of people that have been abused and/or molested and/or fucked over by someone close to them, and I'm no exception. And that's that song." She concluded: "My songs are 90 per cent experience."

Like many of her songs, 'Long Way To Happy' was radio-friendly pop-rock whose instant appeal and hooky melody contrasted almost jarringly with the difficult subject matter. The joy the listener derived from her songs, she said, reflected the cathartic, therapeutic pleasure Pink got from writing them, mirroring the often "heartbreaking" letters she received from her fans, many of them tortured adolescents, which she described as "a kind of weird, random group therapy". Their personal revelations, she admitted, helped her to keep her own torment and unresolved adolescent issues in perspective.

The ballad 'Nobody Knows' allowed her an opportunity to show off her vocal prowess, a gritty, gutsy performance that knocked all the *X Factor* and *American Idol* showboaters into a cocked hat. Described by Pink as the most vulnerable track on the album, it's a song about the emotions that people hide through fear or shame. 'Dear Mr. President' was her open letter to the President of the USA, written in the form of a series of rhetorical questions for George Dubya, each implicating him in such crucial issues as the Iraq war, gay rights, homelessness and drug abuse.

The sixth and title track, 'I'm Not Dead', has been termed by Pink her first "subtle" and "poetic" self-penned song: "Usually it's very much more cartoon-y and blunt, the way I write songs," she has said. "I don't really know diplomacy or subtlety." The song came about towards the end of Pink and producer Billy Mann's musical partnership ("You're my crack of sunlight", as the lyric goes) and expressed the fear she had of another good friendship coming to a close: "We were scared to move on from each other, after seeing how much that little bit of time together changed us, and how scary change is."

'Cuz I Can', one of seven songs lifted off *I'm Not Dead* for single release, was harder to read than the rest of the album, even if it was just as infectious and energetic. A series of boasts set to a stomping, almost glam beat and a piercing one-note guitar squeal that together sounded like Guns N' Roses jamming with The Glitter Band, it opens with Pink outdoing the blingest rappers for macho braggadocio: "I'm P.I.N.K. P.I.M.P. I'm back again, I know y'all missed me," she mocks, going on to brag about how, "I drink more than you, I party harder than you, and my car's faster than yours", at which point she throws up all over her car's 23-inch rims. "Yeah, I talk shit, just deal with it," she sneers, admitting that she's "lived a life of sin" but she doesn't "give a damn".

Finally, there is a staccato falsetto chant of "ice cream, ice cream, we all want ice cream" that sounds like mid-'70s quirk-pop duo Sparks. 'Cuz I Can' has been called "a contrast to the anti-consumerist content of 'Stupid Girls'" but it's more ambiguous than that, Pink delighting in her reputation as a blinged-up bad-ass as much as she appears to be deriding the notion of infamy and conspicuous consumption. Referring to the song, she called herself "a walking contradiction" and "a hypocrite sometimes", which suggests she was as confused about the song's content as some of her listeners.

There were further contradictions expressed on the next track, 'Leave Me Alone (I'm Lonely)', which dealt with paradoxical feelings Pink seems to have vis-à-vis relationships, mainly about how, as soon as she's in one, she wants out, and vice versa. "Go away, come back... Why can't I have it both ways?" she wonders in the song, while elsewhere she compares the relentless sameness of staying with one person to eating the same food from the same restaurant every night. Pink said, "That's how I live my life. I'm a walking conflict." She called the song, with its unforgettable chorus and numerous expletives, "a funny take on 'I love you'... I get really cramped... But then, every girl needs her space."

Pink didn't need any expletives on 'U + Ur Hand' – the ninth track on *I'm Not Dead* was plain rude all over, being an ode to onanism disguised as a kiss-off to a man attempting to seduce the singer. It became a fan favourite before the release of the album, when it was leaked to the Internet. Pink said of 'Runaway' and songs in her catalogue like it that addressed, obliquely or otherwise, her difficult childhood, "It's been especially hard for [my parents] hearing me write about things they never knew about... My mom's like, 'Were you really that angry? Was I really that in denial? Was I really that bad a parent?' 'No, Mom – you were great. You didn't try to run me over with your car. I made it up.' But by writing all of it down and sharing it with the world, I've broken with most of it." Musically, 'Runaway' played the classic grunge trick of going from soft to hard, quiet to loud, as it shifted from the verses to the chorus; you could almost imagine Courtney Love singing it, especially the couplet that rhymes, "I'll meet you in hell" with "I'm not the perfect girl". If she sounded raucous and raunchy on that track, on the next one, the bluesy, acoustic 'The One That Got Away' – which she said was about the classic "Is this the one? Or is the grass really greener?" dilemma – she sounded positively Joplinesque, rasping and bellowing like prime Janis after several high-tar fags.

On 'I Got Money Now', Pink declared that material wealth hadn't made her happy, and she did, indeed, sound pretty miserable on this slow, sombre, downtempo ballad that moves to the beat of a drum machine. Still, for all its solemn atmosphere and sluggish gait, it was hard to feel sorry for her, not least due to lines such as, "I'm so busy buying things and travelling the world I have no time for friends or family."

'Conversations With My 13 Year Old Self' was a guitar-free, overblown affair featuring an orchestra that sounded like a grunge Bond theme with lyrics by a self-obsessed teenage girl, which in a sense it did have – they were lyrics penned by Pink to comfort the angry, angsty 13-year-old Alecia Beth Moore. Pink described the song as a "huge therapy session" aimed at – or for – her "pissed-off, complicated" younger self. Over grandiloquent piano chords and pizzicato strings, Pink explains how the world cared little about her, and even though she'd wished for the best, she'd walked alone. Now she wants to hug her 13-year-old self but if she had managed to deliver these soothing words of solace to the heartbroken teenager, it's not unlikely that the latter would have given the former short shrift. "I needed a hug, and I get it... now," she said. "If I tried to hug my 13-year-old self, she'd try to kick my ass, and then she'd collapse and cry."

Penultimate track 'Fingers' was a change of pace, starting like a techno-pop track before the grungy guitars crashed in. The song was about Pink videotaping herself masturbating. As she said at the time, she probably didn't need to add to the list of songs about masturbation, but she couldn't help herself. Neither could her fans working in advertising in the Far East: the track was picked for use on a cellphone commercial in Taiwan and Korea.

The last song on the album, the "hidden" track 'I Have Seen the Rain', was written by and featured Pink's father, James T. Moore. As Pink explained in the intro to the song, he wrote it "about 40 years ago" when he was a soldier in the Vietnam War, but she said, "It's still relevant today. It's a soldier's cry." Dedicated to "all the vets out there", she said she used to perform it with her dad at "different Vietnam functions". She had always wanted to record it with him, she explained, and learnt to harmonise with it. She said of its recording, "He was so nervous, it was the most adorable experience for a father and daughter to share." With Pink doing her best Joan Baez impression and her dad sounding positively Dylanesque, 'I Have Seen The Rain' seemed to have been dropped from a great height from a completely different album, from an entirely different era, which is why it was a good idea to place it at the end of the album. It was a climax of sorts for Pink, or rather a culmination.

"It was the first song I ever learned, ever heard," she told the *Mail On Sunday*. "When I told Dad I wanted to record it with him, he had tears in his eyes. It's the first time I ever saw my father cry. My father, like every father to a little girl, was my hero when I was growing up. I always told him I would make him proud and buy him a motor-home. I hope I've made him proud and I keep offering him a motor-home but he doesn't want it anymore."

She could probably have afforded a motor-home for every member of her family, close and distant, given how many more sales she racked up with *I'm Not Dead*. Despite still not matching the phenomenal success of *M!ssundaztood*, nevertheless the success of *I'm Not Dead* dwarfs that of lesser acts: to date, it has sold more than six and a half million copies worldwide. The album was a substantial success throughout the world, particularly in Australia. It reached the Top 10 in the US, although it was Pink's lowest-seller there until the success of the single 'U + Ur Hand' reactivated it in early 2007. Although it ranked at a lowly 96th in the list of best-selling albums of the year in the USA during 2007, it sold 126,000 copies in its first week there and debuted at number six, a higher debut position than the two previous Pink albums, even if first-week sales for *I'm Not Dead* were lower. *I'm Not Dead* was initially Pink's lowest-seller in America, and dropped out of the *Billboard* 200 after 23 weeks, but it reappeared at number 198 in late December 2006 and, as of December 2007, it had sold 1.15 million copies there, earning it a platinum certification from the RIAA (Recording Industry Association of America).

In the UK, *I'm Not Dead* debuted at number three after selling almost 40,000 copies and was the ninth best-selling album of 2006, with over 848,000 units shifted; it was certified three times platinum by the BPI (British Phonographic Industry) in January 2007 for shipments to stores of 900,000 copies. By May 2007, the album had surpassed sales of 1 million, had spent 84 weeks in the Top 75 and had sold more than 1.125 million copies; it even re-entered the Top 100 in

October 2007, at number 99. By February 2008, total sales stood at 1,173,564. At the time of writing, that figure should be nearer the 1.2 million sales mark, making *I'm Not Dead* eligible for a quadruple platinum certification.

In Canada, the album debuted at number two with 13,000 copies sold in its first week, and the CRIA (Canadian Recording Industry Association) certified it platinum for shipments of more than 100,000 copies. Bizarrely, in New Zealand, the album reached number one in its 37th week on the chart. It reached the Top 10 in 18 countries, including number one in Germany, and was certified gold, platinum or multi-platinum in more than 17 countries. The statistics detailing its success in Australia are arguably the most impressive. It got to number one twice: the first time after 26 weeks of release, when it became Pink's first Australian number one album; and the second time in its 61st week on the ARIA (Australian Recording Industry Association) chart. The album spent a record 62 consecutive weeks in the Top 10, and as of August 2007, it was certified eight times platinum by ARIA for shipments of 560,000 copies. Pink's most successful album in Australia, it was the second best-selling album of both 2006 and 2007, and the highest-selling album by an American or a female artist in each year. It also yielded five Top 5 singles. Australian-chart.com stated that in August 2008 the album re-entered the charts at number 35, resulting in the album's 94th week on the Australian charts. In its 100th week on the charts *I'm Not Dead* was certified nine-times platinum with shipments of 630,000 copies. As of January 26, 2009, the album was enjoying its 133rd week on the countdown down under, where it was number 18, meaning that *I'm Not Dead* has had the second-longest run in Australian album chart history, one place behind Shania Twain's *Come On Over*.

So much for the album's commercial performance; critically, *I'm Not Dead* had a mixed reaction. Credit was afforded Pink for not, following the relatively unsuccessful *Try This*, "crawling back to what made her a star" – that is, the dancefloor-friendly rock of *M!ssundaztood* or even the shiny urban pop of her debut. Although there were powerfully rhythmic things going on *I'm Not Dead*, it wasn't exactly an attempt to Get The Party Re-Started.

Reviewers tended to like the varied nature of the album, although for "diverse" some said "contrary", even "confused", citing as examples of Pink's changeability the way she attacked "porno paparazzi girls" like Paris Hilton one minute then flaunted her bling on 'Cuz I Can' and shouted out loud that 'I Got Money Now' the next. But it was generally regarded as a good thing that she could swagger and strut and swear like a trooper while also proving herself capable of melancholy and tenderness on consecutive songs. You've got to hand it to an artist, some reviewers noted, who in the space of one album can hurl barbs at the President and a sleazoid in a bar, who can address the tragedy of sexual abuse and then, within minutes, start a chant of "Ice cream, ice cream/We all want ice cream."

The musical eclecticism also appealed to critics, which some detected was the result of collaborating with everyone from Britney Spears hitmaker Max Martin on one track to indie-folk queens the Indigo Girls on a stripped-down protest song the next. Rock disco, fuzztone power pop, blues, folk, lighters-aloft stadium-worthy power ballads and riff-powered electronica – *I'm Not Dead* was either a hotchpotch, evidence of indecision following the mixed reaction to *Try This*, or proof that Pink was, as one reviewer put it, feeling liberated and "making music that's far riskier and stranger than anything else in mainstream pop in 2006."

One writer noted that, for a so-called mainstream record, and despite being the result of her working with her most mainstream producers since her debut album, on *I'm Not Dead* Pink "sounds the strangest she ever has", which he regarded as "a testament to her power as both a musician and a persona." Strongest and strangest: the same writer praised her reach and range – her authentically bluesy performance on 'The One That Got Away', her teasing provocations on 'Stupid Girls' and 'U + Ur Hand', her light pop touch on 'Leave Me Alone (I'm Lonely)'. "In other words," concluded the writer, "she sounds complex: smart, funny, sexy, catchy, and best of all, surprising and unpredictable. This is the third album in a row where she's thrown a curve ball, confounding expectations by delivering a record that's wilder, stronger, and better than the last. *I'm Not Dead* is proof positive that there are few pop musicians more exciting in the 2000s than Pink."

Elsewhere, extra marks were given for the high autobiographical quotient on *I'm Not Dead*, harking back to the diary entries of *M!ssundaztood* and to the way Pink managed to turn dark experiences into challenging but catchy pop-rock. Her vocals were hailed, in at least one instance, as "Grammy-worthy", while she got extra hosannas for dodging pigeonholes. Pink's confessional style of lyric writing elicited comments both positive and negative but most writers decided her brutal honesty and raw emotion were rare in pop.

The *Guardian*, on the release of the album, dramatically presented Pink circa *I'm Not Dead*, following a series of skirmishes – with her parents, with her record company – as facing the biggest battle of them all: saving her career after "her brand of chick rock" had, as the newspaper saw it, fallen out of critical and commercial favour. In this context, the album title, though apparently a "wry smile in the face of her ailing stature", actually turned out to be "one of many post mortems on her desperate past, though this time without the help of song-writer Linda Perry." The broadsheet enjoyed the "gentle melancholia" of 'I Got Money Now', but didn't like the way the "gothic drama" of 'Conversations With My 13 Year Old Self' "blows her teen trauma out of all proportion." Her "party spirit", it decided, "is flat, too, despite some sparkle from Swedish pop maestro Max Martin." Best of all, it decided, was the "haunting" 'I Have Seen The Rain', a "lesson in subtlety and maturity" that "proves that when Pink leaves her damaged inner child in peace, she's still a knockout."

The most esteemed reviewers had the most complimentary things to say. Robert Christgau decided that it was "nice to have this emotional hipster sticking her celebrity cred in the stupid world's face" on *I'm Not Dead* and described 'I've Got Money Now' as "a smarter than usual woe-is-stardom song. Much smarter than usual"; the "Dean" awarded the album a grade A-. Finally, *Rolling Stone* magazine described Pink as a "populist iconoclast" and "ambitious the way Madonna used to be: a mess of contradictions and complications with a knack for making those inner conflicts bolster her art." *I'm Not Dead*, the US rock bible concluded, "swaggers with a cockiness that most dudes in bands can't match. Whether she sings rock, pop, R&B or her usual combination of all three, the 26-year-old Doylestown, Pennsylvania, native is belting more urgently and taking more risks than her pop-radio contemporaries."

Chapter 7

Long Way To Happy

"Sometimes I just head out in my car and turn up somewhere. You do get those moments where you'll be sitting in a class somewhere and some girl or some guy next to you looks at you and you know what's going through their head: 'Isn't that girl Pink or someone?' But I'm not one of those people who can't deal with talking to real people."

Pink's fourth album was a bit of a *Thriller* − with seven tracks lifted off it for single release, it rivalled Michael's Jackson's 1982 opus, which also bequeathed seven singles, as a trove of hits. The first song to be issued as a single from *I'm Not Dead* was 'Stupid Girls', which became a number four hit in Australia and a Top 20 entry in the US charts (see Chapter 5).

The album's second single, 'Who Knew', released in May 2006, initially failed to chart on the *Billboard* Hot 100, but it did finally enter at number 95 in March 2007. It was reissued in the US in June 2007, had reached number nine by mid-

September of that year and gave Pink her eighth Top 10 US single – it is credited, along with the third single 'U + Ur Hand', with re-activating the sales of *I'm Not Dead* there, while others have argued that it helped re-galvanise Pink's career in the States in the wake of *Try This*. It also entered many other countries' Top 10s, including the UK – where it reached number five and remains Pink's longest-running single, spending 26 weeks on the chart – and Australia, where it reached number two, went platinum for sales of over 70,000 copies and was ranked ninth on ARIA's Top 100 singles of 2006.

Billboard raved about the single – which was written by Luke Gottwald, Max Martin and Pink, the same trio responsible for 'U + Ur Hand', and which Pink promoted by performing on *American Idol* – calling it "another cool, smart, plenty passionate melodic jewel about the death of a friend and/or friendship." America's music industry bible decided that it "maintained Pink's stance as the smartest female millennium-era singer/songwriter, dazzling in star quality as alternapop's premier princess."

The single's video was film in spring 2006 in Los Angeles by Dragon, a team comprising Sam Bayer (who directed Nirvana's epochal 'Smells Like Teen Spirit' video), Robert Hales (who did Gnarls Barkley's 'Crazy') and Brian Lazzaro. It features close-ups of Pink at the entrance to a fairground, with a nose ring and pink-tinged platinum blonde hair, as she appears on the front cover of *I'm Not Dead*, while in the background a young man and woman argue over his drug use. At the end, she finds him unconscious after taking an overdose and calls an ambulance, walking away crying as it arrives.

Third single 'U + Ur Hand' took three months to chart on the American Hot 100 and, like its predecessor, peaked at number nine, making it the most successful US single from *I'm*

Not Dead, and her joint-highest-charting song there since 'Just Like A Pill' in 2002. It peaked at number 24 on the Canadian Hot 100, and reached the Top 20 across most of Europe, reaching number 10 in the UK, number four in Germany and number 11 in France. The song went to number five in Australia, where it was certified platinum for sales of 70,000 copies. It was ranked at number 25 on ARIA's Top 100 Singles of 2006.

As she admitted in the documentary, *The Making Of The U + Ur Hand Video*, she found it annoying to be approached so often by men while she was out dancing with friends in a club, especially when, after turning them down, they immediately used it as an excuse to question her sexuality: "When you turn a boy down in a club you are automatically a lesbian, according to them," she scowled. But she also saw the funny side. Apparently, she heard one hapless suitor declare, "Oh well, it's just me and my hand tonight" after a girl turned him down. In fact, Pink found it so amusing that she wrote a song about it.

Not everyone got the joke, but because of its references to masturbation it caused quite a stir in the States, and some radio stations refused to play it. For her *American Idol* performance, she was asked to change the title and lyric to 'U + Ur Heart', but she reportedly said, "You want me to rewrite my song for you. For American fucking Idol? What does that even mean, how do you have sex with your heart?" The TV show won the argument, however, and she performed 'Who Knew' instead.

'U + Ur Hand' was described as "a female anthem" and "very fitting to people who are sick of getting hit on by guys at the club, and want to give them a nice buzz off." *Rolling Stone* opined that Pink "sets a proudly bitchy tone in the song", while the *Guardian* were ambiguous in their praise, saying, "The pithy put-downs make bearable the sudden shift from classy beats to lumpen power pop".

Dave Meyers directed the 'U + Ur Hand' video, as he did the one for 'Stupid Girls'. It was shot in Sun Valley, California, at the Haziza Gallery in Los Angeles, at La Center Studios and at the Hollywood Roosevelt Hotel in Hollywood, California in December 2005. Pink is shown in a variety of poses and guises, each with their own character names such as "Baby Red Knuckles", "Rocker Bikerboy" and "Hard Candy": one was a goth-esque vamp in long black wig, another a punky sprite with neon red hair. Pink commented that it took four hours of make-up and one hour of shooting for every different look in the video. Despite the colourful nature of the short there were no allusions to self-pleasuring.

The fourth single, 'Nobody Knows', was released outside the US and reached the Top 40 in the UK (where it was Pink's lowest-peaking single up to that point, and the first *I'm Not Dead* single to miss the Top 10), Ireland and Australia. Strangely, it reached number 27 in all three countries, although it was the only physical single from *I'm Not Dead* to not make the Top Five on the Australian chart. Then again, at one point there were three Pink singles – 'Who Knew', 'U + Ur Hand' and 'Nobody Knows' – in the Australian Top 50. It also reached number 17 in Germany.

The video was shot in London by Jake Nava, who directed the MOBO-nominated 'Crazy In Love' for Beyoncé. A gloomy affair, everything is darkly lit. Pink is shown variously trashing her bedroom in a hotel (actually The May Fair, set in the heart of the capital's plush Mayfair district), sitting crouched despairingly in the foetal position in the shower, walking down a rain-lashed street past a couple in love and some drunks, wailing in the back of a taxi and, at the end, singing to an empty auditorium, pretending to perform. It was a stylish, lugubrious short that proved an effective visual counterpoint to the song.

Single number five from *I'm Not Dead* was 'Dear Mr. President', Pink's politically charged team-up with the Indigo Girls. The lesbian cult duo were invited to record it alongside her because they "really believed in the song" and because Pink "worshipped the ground they walked on". For Indigo Girl Amy Ray, the feeling was entirely mutual: "I've always admired her punch in the Top 40 world, her gat gun approach," said Ray. "It's a great song that we need right now, and it's asking some really important questions." Pink concurred, calling 'Dear Mr. President' one of the most important songs she had ever written (or rather, co-written with Max Martin). She explained that she wrote it on Martin Luther King Day in 2005. "I read *The New York Times* every day and watch the news," she told a reporter. "And I was completely disgusted with it. I just felt like I needed to write a song. So I walked into the studio and said, 'I want to get political.'"

In Belgium an acoustic version of the song was released as a downloadable single in late 2006. The single was recorded at a showcase for Q-music, a Belgian radio station. It held the number one spot on the Ultratop 50 Chart for four weeks, becoming the first download-only song to reach number one. Elsewhere in Europe, it reached number one in Austria, the Top Five in Switzerland and Germany (where it was certified gold), and the Top 40 in the Netherlands.

In the UK, it was released as a download-only single, where it reached the Top 40 (it was also available in physical form as an import CD). Down Under, it went Top 40 in New Zealand and peaked at number five in Australia, where it became the fifth Top Five hit from *I'm Not Dead*. The single was released in special two-disc CD form commemorating Pink's I'm Not Dead Tour in Australia.

While 'Dear Mr. President' was not released in the US

because Pink feared its impact would be diminished and seen as a mere publicity stunt, many American radio stations played the song. They could hardly ignore it, official release as a single or not. When *I'm Not Dead* was issued in April 2006, the track attracted considerable attention for its attack on George W. Bush and its questioning of his policies on such controversial issues as war ("Let me tell you about hard work/Rebuilding your house after the bombs took them away"), the homeless ("What do you feel when you see all the homeless on the street?"), abortion ("What kind of father would take his own daughter's rights away?"), drug abuse ("You've come a long way from whiskey and cocaine"), the war in Iraq ("How do you feel when a mother has no chance to say goodbye?") and homosexuality (ironically, former Vice President Dick Cheney didn't accept gay rights either, despite his own daughter being a lesbian). "When you look in the mirror," Pink asked Bush in the song, "are you proud?" In an interview with MTV News Pink said she hoped the President heard the song and that "[he] is proud of the fact that we live in a country where people can do things like that, where we can have dissent, talk, communicate and share our opinions."

Like the video for next single 'Leave Me Alone (I'm Lonely)', the 'Dear Mr. President' video caught Pink live on the *I'm Not Dead* tour, specifically performing in London at Wembley Arena (later caught for posterity on the tour DVD *Pink: Live From Wembley Arena*). Pink is shown at the front of the stage with her backing vocalists and an acoustic guitar, singing the song while, on giant screens behind her, images appeared of Bush along with child casualties of the Iraq war, coffins with American flags over them (suggesting soldiers who had died during the conflict), victims of Hurricane Katrina and more.

A pink guitar, Janis Joplin and Bob Marley for inspiration, 2003. (F. SCOTT SCHAFER/CORBISOUTLINE)

Pink accepts her award onstage at the 2006 MTV Video Music Awards at Radio City Music Hall, New York City. (FRANK MICELOTTA/GETTY IMAGES)

MTV VJ Damien Fahey and singer Pink appear on MTV's *Total Request Live*, April 5, 2006, New York City. (PETER KRAMER/GETTY IMAGES)

Pink on an amusement park ride after shooting the new video for 'Who Knew', April 2006, in Los Angeles. (FRANK MICELOTTA/GETTY IMAGES FOR LA FACE RECORDS)

Pink on stage at the opening concert of her 'I'm Not Dead' European tour at Hallen Stadion, Zurich, Switzerland, September 27, 2006. (GETTY IMAGES)

Pink wields a chain saw while filming the video for 'So What', August 6, 2008, Los Angeles. The video was directed by Dave Myers. (FRANK MICELOTTA/GETTY IMAGES FOR SONY BMG)

Pink crosses her fingers as the awards are announced on stage during the third annual MTV Australia Video Music Awards at Acer Arena Sydney, Australia, on April 29, 2007. (KRISTIAN DOWLING/GETTY IMAGES)

Carey Hart and Pink at the 49th Annual Grammy Awards in Los Angeles, February 2007, when she was nominated as Best Female Pop Vocal Performance for 'Stupid Girls'. (KEVIN MAZUR/WIREIMAGE)

Pink performs on the film set of the latest T-Mobile ad in Trafalgar Square, London, April, 2009.
(DANNY MARTINDALE/WIREIMAGE)

Pink backstage at the 2008 MTV Video Music Awards at Paramount Pictures Studios, Los Angeles, September 2008. (KEVIN MAZUR/WIREIMAGE)

Pink in May, 2006. (GEORGE HOLZ / CONTOURPHOTOS.COM)

In 2003, when Natalie Maines of the Texas-based female country trio Dixie Chicks said on stage in London that they were ashamed that the President of the US was from their home state, there was a serious controversy, largely stirred up by right wing media in their home country. As a result, many in America boycotted the group's concerts, there were accusations that they were unpatriotic and there were even public gatherings where their albums were destroyed in protest. Three years later it would seem that Pink could stage a far more overt public criticism of Bush yet it was largely ignored. This may have been because pop (and R&B) are regarded as less 'serious' mediums than country or rock, but also – probably – because by this time the world had woken up to the mistakes made by President Bush's administration and Pink was merely adding to an overwhelming barrage of worldwide criticism aimed at Bush and his cronies.

The sixth *I'm Not Dead* single, 'Leave Me Alone (I'm Lonely)', was released in 2007 as a physical CD in Australia, and as a download-only EP in Britain (although certain European countries received a physical CD release) along with 'Dear Mr. President' featuring live versions of both songs. It was put on the B-list at Radio 1 and debuted at number 60 on the charts, eventually rising to number 34, Pink's lowest-peaking UK single up to that point. In Australia it debuted at number 11 and peaked at number five; the single also reached the Top Five in New Zealand where it was certified gold in October 2008, selling over 7,500 copies. The video for the single comprised footage from Pink's I'm Not Dead Tour, including shots of her performing not just 'Leave Me Alone' but also 'Stupid Girls', 'Fingers', 'The One That Got Away' and 'U + Ur Hand'.

Finally, the seventh single, 'Cuz I Can', was released as a

digital download in Australia, where it peaked at number 14 on the digital tracks chart (on its release in New Zealand, it became the first single to chart on download sales alone, peaking at number 29). The video was first seen on Australian television on October 5, 2007 and was another live performance from the I'm Not Dead Tour. The performance, which was the show opener for the tour, featured dancers in underwear moving with military precision as Pink strutted about imperiously in shades and an impressively tall military-style cap.

It made sense for Australia to have been treated to the video exclusive. After all, of its six-million-plus worldwide sales, *I'm Not Dead* has sold over 630,000 copies there, comparing quite favourably with the 1.3 million in the far more densely populated USA. But then, Pink has always been very popular in Australia, and the nine-times-platinum *I'm Not Dead* album was no exception, with six Top Five singles and a record-breaking 62 weeks in the Top 10. In June 2008, the album returned to the Australian Top 40 and was still there in November 2008 where it sat at number 15, meaning that, up to that point, it had racked up an incredible total of 110 weeks in the Australian Top 40.

To further promote *I'm Not Dead* and sustain sales of the album, Pink embarked on the I'm Not Dead Tour, for which ticket sales in Australia were particularly high – she sold approximately 307,000 tickets there, giving her the record for the biggest-ever concert attendance in that country for an arena tour by a female artist. Pink broke another record by being the only female artist to play seven consecutive sold-out shows in Sydney. Sony BMG Australia released a special tour edition of *I'm Not Dead* in March 2007, containing the original album plus two bonus tracks and a DVD featuring live performances and various music videos. Pink began her North American I'm Not Dead Tour in June 2006 in Chicago and it ended in Dallas after 20 shows. She started her European tour in September of the same year in Istanbul; it ran for 52 shows and ended in Milan in December. A DVD of a concert on this leg of the tour, *Pink: Live from Wembley Arena*, was released in April 2007. Pink then returned to the US to accompany Justin Timberlake on the American leg of his FutureSex/LoveShow tour.

Pink was also chosen to sing the theme song for NBC Sunday Night Football, 'Waiting All Day For Sunday Night', a take on 'I Hate Myself For Lovin' You' by Joan Jett. She contributed a cover of Rufus' soul standard 'Tell Me Something Good' to the soundtrack of the film *Happy Feet*, and lent her name to PlayStation to promote the PSP, a special pink edition of which was released. Pink received the 2006 *Glamour Magazine* award for International Solo Artist of the Year, and in 2007 she won the MTV Australia Video Music Award for Best Female Artist as well as the Nickelodeon Kids' Choice Award (in Australia) for Favourite International.

Elsewhere in the bid to prolong the afterlife of *I'm Not Dead*, another track from the album, 'Long Way To Happy', was featured in an episode of MTV's *The Hills*, 'Who Knew' was used in promotion for the ABC television show *October Road* in March 2007, the title track was used in an episode of the last season of the TV show *Charmed* and 'Dear Mr. President' aired at the end of the fourth season finale of the series *The L Word*. In December 2007, an edition of the album titled *I'm Not Dead: Platinum Edition* was released.

Also during this period Pink sang on the Indigo Girls album *Despite Our Differences*. She appeared on India Arie's song 'I Am Not My Hair' and featured in the Lifetime

Television film *Why I Wore Lipstick To My Mastectomy*. She wrote a song called 'I Will' for Natalia's third album, *Everything & More*. 'Outside Of You', another song she co-wrote, was recorded by dance-pop diva Hilary Duff and released on her 2007 album *Dignity*. She recorded a song with Annie Lennox and 22 other female acts, including Madonna, Fergie, Dido and Sugababes, for Lennox's fourth solo studio album, *Songs Of Mass Destruction*. Titled 'Sing', the track was written as an anthem for HIV/AIDS, according to Lennox's official site. In December 2007, a special edition Pink Box, comprising her second to fourth albums and the DVD Live in Europe, was released in Australia, reached the Top 20 on the albums chart and was certified gold, selling over 35,000 copies.

I'm Not Dead was, in a sense, kept alive for almost two years, a long time for an artist's fourth album, testament to Pink's enduring popularity and widespread appeal.

Notwithstanding her and Australia's mutual appreciation society over the years, Pink did have a run-in with a section of the country over her campaigning nature, specifically in the area of cruelty to animals, of which she has a history (see Chapter 5). Around this time, in conjunction with animal rights organisation PETA, after selling out her Australian tour dates, she criticised the Australian wool industry over its use of mulesing, the removal of strips of wool-bearing skin from around the breech (buttocks) of a sheep, a common practice in Australia. In January 2007, however, she stated that she had been misled by PETA about mulesing and that she had not done enough research before lending her name to the campaign. Her zealous nature also led to an appearance in an advertisement for PETA's anti-fur campaign and a headlining concert in Cardiff, Wales, in August 2007 called PAW (Party for Animals Worldwide).

These were just two examples of Pink's commitment to causes beyond the realm of rock and pop. She has been involved with numerous charities over the years including one called Phoenix Vert, the Human Rights Campaign, the ONE Campaign, the Prince's Trust, the New York Restoration Project, the Run for the Cure Foundation, Save the Children, Take Back the Night, UNICEF and the World Society for the Protection of Animals.

In May 2008 she was officially recognised as an advocate for the RSPCA in Australia and in February 2009 she announced that she was donating $250,000 to the Red Cross Bushfire Appeal to aid the victims of the bushfires that swept through the Australian state of Victoria earlier that month, which killed more than 208 people, claiming that she wanted to make "a tangible expression of support".

Pink has also been involved in Kentucky Fried Cruelty, a PETA-backed campaign that began in 2001, seeking to change the fast-food outlet's treatment of chickens raised for its restaurants. KFC is the fourth restaurant chain to have been targeted by the animal rights organisation, following similar campaigns against Burger King and McDonald's.

Ironically, when she was younger, Pink had a year-long stint at a McDonald's franchise in her home town of Doylestown in Pennsylvania. She has said of this grim period in her life, "That job sucked." She also admitted she was still haunted by memories of working there: "Sometimes I dream I am back there, broke and working at McDonald's. It's like the worst nightmare because I would never want to be back there. I've worked hard to get where I am."

In November 2006, Pink mentioned in the *News Of The World* that she was disgusted with fellow singer Beyoncé for wearing fur, and she still stood by that remark a year later.

"I stand by what I say about any fur-wearing idiot, yes," she said, typically forthright. "I work with PETA all the time. I will always side with the animals. I've always been into animal rights. I had a year where I forgot and lost the plot completely but I came back. PETA makes it fun and they get things done. They don't just talk about it." Her intention, she said, was to one day open an animal sanctuary. "I would probably need to be closer to the countries that need the animal sanctuaries most," she said, "such as Mexico or Puerto Rico." She said that she wanted to set up a "mobile vet unit for spaying and neutering", saying that she had already written letters to the nations in question, informing them that she would "personally match whatever money they put in." She added: "I'm serious about it."

Rather than spending her free time hobnobbing with the Hollywood glitterati, she was more likely, she added, to holiday on her own in far-flung places, usually with some educational component.

"I love going to places like a Kenyan ranch or any sort of retreat," she told journalist Louise Gannon. She would go there on her own and use it as an opportunity to take a course in anything from hypnotherapy and meditation to basket-weaving. "Sometimes I just head out in my car and turn up somewhere," she said. "You do get those moments where you'll be sitting in a class somewhere and some girl or some guy next to you looks at you and you know what's going through their head: 'Isn't that girl Pink or someone?' But I'm not one of those people who can't deal with talking to real people." In fact, she said, she actually preferred the company of non-celebrities. Best of all, however, was being alone. Isolation is, to Pink, a treasure and a joy. "The best thing about being on my own is reading," she revealed. "I read all the time. I love it.

My fantasy would be to be locked in a library. I'd be very, very happy."

For all her reputation for being an ex-skatepunk turned hellraising tattooed rock chick with a penchant for handguns, motorbikes and narcotics (with the list of drugs she'd sampled over the years including, as she told Q magazine, acid, ketamine, ecstasy, PCP and crystal meth), there is actually a large part of Pink's character that veers towards zen earth mother. As much as she's into partying and living large, she's also into long periods of quiet contemplation and the pursuit of calm. She likes nothing more than to sit in front of the TV and weep along with a glass of wine to an old-fashioned chick-flick like *Love Story*. She even had, at one point, an organic vegetable garden with four raised beds where she grew cucumbers, tomatoes, melons, jalapeño peppers, spinach, kale and chillies. "I also grow sunflowers, marigolds and herbs like basil and marjoram," she said. "I like to get out there in my wellies. I'm full-on." She decided that it was "very punk rock" to be "out in a yard growing your own food."

Pink has always been a firm believer in the dictum that "actions speak louder than words". "I really respect women who are responsible and smart and thinkers and activists and doers," she has said. Not that she's against the odd spot of peaceful navel-gazing, especially faced with all the iniquities she sees in the world around her.

"I want to understand why everyone hates each other," she told *The Big Issue*. Given the state of things, she added, with all the wars and the ecological and financial crises, she was concerned about bringing children into such a harsh, unforgiving world. "It's very daunting and I try not to say it out loud because all my friends have babies so I don't want to freak them out, but – what the fuck? Will there even be a planet when they're 40?" She revealed that she would not be against Doing A Madonna and adopting a baby orphan at some stage from an impoverished Third World country. "I'm of the school of thought that there are kids here who need rescuing, so why not do that and give them a great life?" she wondered out loud. "There are a lot of kids already on this planet that need help, food and love."

Pink worried a lot, she said, about the meaning of life, and whether the quest for eternal happiness was a remote possibility. She admitted to her tendency to sit around, listening to "farty French music", and dreaming of the day when she would have time to study psychology, master the violin and learn Spanish and French. She said she also enjoyed reading philosophical tracts such as *The God Of Small Things* by Arundhati Roy, *Pillars Of The Earth* by Ken Follett and Huston Smith's comparative study of belief systems, *The World's Religions*. "Me and my friends sit around drinking whiskey, trying to find our truth. You know, to love and be loved, and figuring out how to find out who the fuck we are. And every time we use sex or a fucking glass pipe or drink we get further from the truth. So how do you feel free and yummy to the point where it actually lasts and you remember it?"

Pink is virtually synonymous with exuberance, high energy and bright pop colour, but she's also the queen of teen angst and solipsist introspection. It's hardly surprising, then, that she has been in therapy, even if she struggled to take it seriously. "I either say nothing or tell jokes," she has said. "There was this one therapist who told me, 'I really like you and think you're really funny, but when are you going to start telling me the truth?' I just said, 'Fine. I'm going to write a song and then I'm gonna kill myself.'" For Pink, therapy "doesn't really work", even if she does get a perverse kick out of putting herself "in the most uncomfortable situations", reasoning that, "If you call it, you take the sting out of it."

Pink is nothing if not a fascinating potential case study for psychiatrists. Her two female artist role models are hard-living bad girl Janis Joplin and mainstream showbiz diva Bette Midler. She's the pop star who wrote 'Stupid Girls' who has said, "I'm a stupid girl, too." She's the pacifist who's into Swat team training and shooting rifles. She's the ex-gymnast and fitness fanatic who punished her body with narcotics as a teenager. She's the fierce advocate for letting people be themselves who has managed to have very public spats with Christina Aguilera and Paris Hilton purely because she didn't like the way they were. She's the exhibitionist who turned down the opportunity to snog Madonna at the 2003 MTV Awards so that her rival, Britney Spears, had to step into the breach instead. She's the self-styled motorcycle-riding butch girl whose friends have told her, "C'mon, admit it, you're a dyke", whose only truly public affair has been with a man. And she's the in-yer-face gregarious loudmouth who secretly harbours a desire for a lifetime commitment, a conventional relationship and the sort of white-picket-fence existence that she seemed to rebel against years ago in Doylestown.

Make that a *really* fascinating potential case study for psychiatrists.

Chapter 8

Save My Life

"Carey knows how psychotic I am. He spent six and a half years with me. A year with me is like dog years. I definitely bring crazy to the table. How can you not, riding a lawnmower down Sunset Boulevard when people are flicking you off?"

Pink had done many things during her career, but she hadn't had a boyfriend. She did have one just before she became famous – between the ages of 15 and 21, she went out with a young father of one, but the relationship foundered when she became successful, although not because he had a daughter. Indeed, as she told the *Guardian*, his child kept the affair going longer than it might have otherwise. "It wasn't particularly happy," she said of the relationship. But, she confided, she was an integral part of the girl's upbringing. "It had a lot to do with his daughter," she said of the reason for it lasting longer than it should. "She was three when we met and I raised her until she was nine. People staying together for kids," she added, referencing her parents' divorce, "is not always healthy, which I know first-hand, but I was very attached to her."

Until she met professional motocross racer (and part-time tattoo parlour entrepreneur) Carey Hart at the 2001 X Games in Philadelphia – in fact even during their relationship and afterwards – there were still questions raised about Pink's sexual orientation. Not that she was remotely cagey or uncomfortable when confronted about the subject, sometimes laughing about fancying both Johnny Depp and Vanessa Paradis. Many presumed that Pink was at least bisexual, or even a lesbian, neither of which intimation offended her in the slightest. "Of course not," she would say. "Most of my friends are lesbians. When I first appeared people couldn't figure out whether I was gay, straight, black, white or whatever, and I loved that. I loved the fact it scares people."

"A lot of my friends are gay and I'm not a girly-girl," she told *The Big Issue*. "I'm kinda butch; I tell it like it is. I ride a motorcycle and my best friend's a lesbian, but none of that bothers me at all." The prospect of being gay, she said, was never a concern. "I remember being a teenager and sexuality wasn't my issue." The only existential dilemmas that troubled her were, she joked, such matters as, "Is there life beyond High School? Should I kill myself now?"

With her honed, strong, sinewy body and raspy, sardonic voice ("she could out-drawl Clint Eastwood," observed one interviewer), Pink has frequently been described as "masculine". This never bothered her, either, although she has said of the prospect of having male genitalia, "I wouldn't like something swinging between my legs", adding that she loved being female and all that it entailed, especially after she turned 25. "I feel I'm not a girl anymore," she commented. "I'm a woman, and I want to know how to use that power."

Pink was certainly the one in charge when it came to taking her relationship with the motocross superstar, who she had been dating for four years, to the next level. It was she who proposed to Hart, apparently because of his strength of character and his prowess in the bedroom: "The energy between me and Carey is palpable. It will always be that way," Pink told *Look* magazine. "It's like two alphas in a room who just want to rip each other's clothes off. He is incredible in the bedroom, too. I think that's why I proposed!"

The unorthodox proposal came in late 2005 during one of his pit boarding races in Mammoth Lakes, California. Emboldened by a large vodka and Red Bull, she held up a sign that read, "Will you marry me?" On the other side was written, "I'm Serious!" After the Mohican-haired biker read it, he almost crashed into a siding. She and Hart tied the knot in a ceremony on a beach in Costa Rica on January 7, 2006 at sunset. The song chosen for Pink's walk down the aisle, for which she wore a dress designed by the woman responsible for Britney Spears' wedding dress, was Billy Joel's 'She's Always A Woman'. The wedding cake featured models of the bride and groom on motocross bikes while the couple sported matching "Tru Luv" tattoos on their wrists. During their wedding vows, Hart apparently thanked the bottle of Absolut vodka that gave Pink the courage to propose. Pink described the wedding – attended by family, friends and the odd celeb such as Lisa Marie Presley – as "the best weekend of my life".

The Pink-Hart union soon turned out to be as unconventional as might have been expected, given the nature of their careers, what with her being away on tour and him busy freestyling on bikes around the world; nevertheless, the intention was to be a proper ordinary married couple because, as the singer said of her new husband, "I believe him." Pink declared that, as soon as she got married, her nurturing, domestic side emerged and she felt a sudden desire to make cupcakes for hubbie and run along the beach with her dogs. "Inside of me there's a housewife desperate to get out," she said. She believed the biggest misconception about her was that she was a "very serious, bitter, angry, scary, feminist girl". On the contrary, she said: "I don't think so. I just want to go home and play in my garden."

She even planned to have children with Hart: "If I'm lucky – if I'm blessed. One day. But Carey's a tattooed dirt-bike dude." When asked what potential little Pink-Harts could possibly find to rebel against, she replied, "'Oooh – tattoos are gross, Dad!' 'Mom, I want to play chess! I want to do ballet!'" She said she looked forward to that moment. "That'd be nice. That's the kind of kids I want. I don't want a kid anything like me. If I have a girl like me, someone's gonna have to bury me early. Or her!"

Unfortunately, however, the fairytale marriage didn't last much more than a couple of years and, in February 2008, after months of speculation, the couple announced that they were to separate, although Pink was quick to say that she and Hart were "friends whether we are married or not". The unconventional nature of their relationship began to emerge, and it transpired that the couple had separate homes – his in Las Vegas, hers in LA – while conjugal meet-ups during their two-year marriage were infrequent due to their jet-setting lives. And yet Pink's publicist insisted: "This decision was made by best friends with a huge amount of love and respect for one another."

By March 2008, the papers were already reporting that, while Pink's estranged husband was in Las Vegas, the "newly single pop singer was living it up in West Hollywood –

hanging with some pals and getting frisky onstage with a hair rocker!" The 28-year-old pop star, it was noted, was spotted enjoying herself alongside other celebrities (including actor Michael Rappaport) at the Key Club for a performance from tongue-in-cheek rockers Metal Skool. After stepping onstage to join the group, Pink was spotted hugging "a sweaty, heavily hair-sprayed member of the band".

Then again, in July of that year stories began to appear focusing on how the couple were still good friends. "We're still very much on good terms," Pink said. "We don't get jealous but then we're not [yet] at the place where we're meeting other girlfriends and boyfriends. [But] I'm not with him so he can do whatever he wants." As for Hart, he told *People* maga-zine at the opening of his new Las Vegas club, Wasted Space, in the Hard Rock Hotel: "We talk all the time and try to stay connected as much as possible. It's a tough situation to be in but I love her to death." And despite no longer being a couple, Hart confessed how much he missed his ex. "I miss everything about her," he said, adding that, in the wake of their split, he had become "a workaholic", working "19 hours a day." He also admitted that he wasn't yet ready to move on – "I'm not in any rush to get back into a relationship," he said – and that he still hoped for a reunion with Pink. "I would like to have wishful thinking and say, 'Yes.' Only time will tell." Meanwhile, his plan was to keep the lines of communication open – "and who knows," he said, "what will happen when we get older... For the next three years, though, we're both extremely busy peo-ple so it's tough." He revealed, too, that he harboured dreams of being a dad. "I am [on a time clock]," he said. "I don't want to do it past 35. My body is so destroyed, and I want to be a fun, young dad, not crippled and beat up. So I'd like to have kids by 35. I want 'em!"

Pink spoke openly about her feelings in the wake of the break-up in *Cosmopolitan*. She revealed that she felt disappointed at the collapse of her marriage, saying, "I wanted the fairytale and we didn't quite make it." However, she said that she didn't have any regrets and that she was "loving every second" of single life, relishing her down time at her home in Malibu, exercising on the beach and "hanging out with close friends". She pointed out that, just because she was single it didn't mean that there were not men in her life. "For me," she said, "it's all about the eye candy. I'm enjoying window shopping!" She didn't have a type when it came to men, she said: "I've dated hot surfers, dirty rockers, men in suits... If a guy's got it, he's got it. I think attraction is all about charisma and a connection you can't put your finger on." She concluded that she was "in a great place mentally right now" as well as being a firm believer in the adage, "I felt bad for the man with no shoes until I met the man with no feet". "There will," she said, "always be somebody worse off and I know how fortunate I am."

There were further insights into Pink's love life a month or so later when she revealed that she had never been on a date and preferred meeting men in less pressurised situations, despite friends' attempts to set her up with acquaintances of theirs. She said ideally she would meet men in natural situations such as at a show or a barbecue. "I meet boys all over the place," she said. "It's just that I don't ever go on dates. I have never been on a date. I don't believe in that, it has to be organic... I have never met anybody in a bar. Lately I have been hearing from a lot of people, like married couples, who have met in a bar. I'm always amazed. So maybe that is where I am going wrong." Besides, she said, dates weren't for her right now because she was still not over her ex. "I'm still in love with him," she told *People* magazine. "There's no one cuter than Carey. I'm not looking for anyone else right now." She also disclosed that their split was over a disagreement about starting a family. She said: "What happened was between us. But it wasn't a nasty thing. It was, 'Let's have babies one day, but not now. Let's just be cool.'"

Pink gave different reasons for the split in other interviews. In one she said it was simply because she could not deal with being a kept woman. "We all get into playing roles when we're in a relationship," she told journalist Gabrielle Donnelly. "'I'm the wife, you're the husband.' Well, those roles didn't work out for us. It doesn't mean we don't love each other very much, and even though the marriage roles didn't work, we're still trying to figure out which roles do." In another she put the breakup down to her capricious nature. "I can be crazy and out-there. I'd drive Carey crazy when he had fights: 'Go away... come back... go away... come back.' I'm a walking conflict. And you know what really makes Carey mad? We'll be having a passionate fight and he'll be building up to his point when I'll start laughing and say: 'Can you just come over here and kiss me?' That makes him so angry!" Elsewhere she blamed their conflicting work schedules, explaining that they were sometimes lucky to only see each other once a month. "It's such a cliché when you talk about a Hollywood divorce, but the scheduling did get very hard. And it seemed that I was always the one left in charge of it. I got tired of being Schedule Woman."

And yet for all this talk of an amicable, harmonious parting, of their "authentic connection" and ability to love each other without the possessiveness of a monogamous relationship, by summer 2008, rumours began to spread that Pink was so badly affected by the split with Hart, that she was considering turning to Scientology, encouraged by her actress/musician friends

Kirstie Alley, Lisa Marie Presley and Juliette Lewis, all devout followers of the controversial belief system. "Pink is in the beginning stages of checking out the religion," a source told America's *Star* magazine. "But she has taken to it and she wants to get more involved."

The impression given by reports and general hearsay was that Pink had been left either bereft or at least a little winded by her divorce from Hart. But the facts told quite a different story. Because in August 2008, her brand new single, 'So What', the first release from her forthcoming fifth album, rather than being a miserable dirge of a ballad, showed that the singer, on the eve of her 29th birthday, was in a more irrepressible and preternaturally exuberant mood than ever.

Any suggestions that she was feeling downhearted and depressed were somewhat contradicted by the fearsome energy of the music and the combative nature of the lyric. It opened with a joke – a pretty funny, one, at that: "I guess I just lost my husband/I don't know where he went" – and proceeded from there. "So I'm gonna drink my money/I'm not gonna pay his rent (nope)," roared her Autotuned voice. "I've got a brand new attitude/And I'm gonna wear it tonight/I'm gonna get in trouble/I wanna start a fight." The chorus was even more assertive and belligerent, declaring in no uncertain terms, "So what, I'm still a rock star/I got my rock moves/And I don't need you/And guess what?/I'm havin' more fun." Not that there was any announcement that this was, in fact, an autobiographical account of her break-up with Hart, but the sense was strong that this was Pink exorcising the spectre of her failed marriage. "And now that we're done/I'm gonna show you tonight/I'm alright/I'm just fine," she railed in the song, going on to affirm that she was having more fun alone and to dismiss the subject of her derision as a "tool". It was like a punk-pop version of that I-don't-need-a-man disco staple, 'I Will Survive'.

Of course, this being Pink, nothing was that simple. She left a clue about the truth of the situation on her MySpace for her fans shortly after the song went to radio, saying of it: "Glad you likey's. And don't worry – Carey likey's too. We are insane."

It transpired that Hart was in on the joke, because his was one of the first faces you saw in the video (and one of the last), a fast-paced, fun-packed affair that featured, among other things, Pink getting tattooed, setting her hair on fire, taking a chainsaw to a tree bearing the names "Alecia + Carey" in a love heart, fighting with a store clerk and riding down a busy Los Angeles street on a lawnmower while drinking alcohol. "This video was too much fun," she wrote on her blog. "If you ever get a chance to drive a lawnmower down Sunset Blvd. – I highly suggest it."

So was 'So What' – which was written by Pink earlier that year in Stockholm while merry from the effects of "really good wine" – really autobiographical? In interviews, the singer denied that it was, and that only a few aspects of the song were based on real events or experiences. Many assumed the video provided an insight into her relationship with Carey Hart and dealt with her separation and pending divorce.

It may have captured Pink as a trouble-maker, but the 'So What' video was hardly an attempt to stir things up between her and her estranged husband, who she once described as "the only person in the world who totally gets me"; indeed, the closing shot was of the pair grinning while she blew a raspberry at the camera. Pink revealed that she had tricked Hart into appearing in the video, explaining to Radio 1 DJ Chris Moyles how it happened and admitting that they were still the best of friends.

"I think it's brilliant," she said. "He hadn't heard the song before he showed up for the video. He was like, 'Yeah, I'll be in the video, whatever.' He's a good sport; he knows how psychotic I am. He spent six and a half years with me. A year with me is like dog years." She said of the filming of 'So What', "It was so much fun – bittersweet, but really fun. I definitely bring crazy to the table. How can you not, riding a lawnmower down Sunset Boulevard when people are flicking you off? I know how to spend my Monday morning." It was the 'So What' video, said Pink, that enabled her to work out a healthy post-divorce relationship with her ex-husband. "It's helped both of us. The fact we can still laugh together and piss each other off, roll our eyes at each other, throw our hands up in the air and at the end of the day it's good – we're solid."

Another good, solid relationship enjoyed by Pink was with Dave Meyers, who worked on the videos for 'U + Ur Hand' and 'Stupid Girls', and who was once again drafted in to direct the short for 'So What'. Indeed, Pink has been something of a muse for Meyers, who has, over the years, directed the videos for 'There You Go', 'Most Girls', 'You Make Me Sick', 'Get The Party Started', 'Don't Let Me Get Me' and the *Charlie's Angels: Full Throttle* track 'Feel Good Time'. The video for her 18th single was the liveliest, most fast-paced to date of the Pink-Meyers team-ups. But even Pink blanched at one of the scenes. Of the numerous set-ups – sitting in a bar after losing her table to blonde bimbo Jessica Simpson and riding a motorbike while a newly wedded couple in a car pull up beside her, causing her to jealously pop the happy newlyweds' blown-up condoms used to decorate the vehicle – the one where she had to strip on a red carpet, surrounded by paparazzi snapping photos of her as she does choreography from Michael Jackson's video for *Thriller* naked caused the most embarrassment. Not surprisingly, a bit of Dutch courage was in order.

"I wasn't comfortable with the 'cookies' bit," she said, refer-ring to her exposed genitalia (which were actually blurred in the film). "I put some underwear on, but I'm kind of an exhi-bitionist, too. I had a shot of tequila. It was 7am, it was the first shot of the second morning. The first shot of the video was me and Carey. Had a beer..."

She probably had another drink when she saw how ecstati-cally the single was received. Commercially, it was Pink's biggest success to date, peaking at number one in 11 countries around the world, including Australia, Canada, Germany, and Ireland as well as the UK and the US. It debuted at number nine on the *Billboard* Hot 100 on August 26, 2008, making it Pink's highest debut to date on the chart. The song subse-quently peaked at number one on September 16, making it her first solo chart-topper – ahead of Kid Rock's 'All Summer Long' and 'Just Dance' by Lady GaGa – and second overall after 'Lady Marmalade', her collaboration with Christina Aguilera, Mýa, and Lil' Kim. It was Pink's ninth Top 10 hit on the chart, and her third consecutive. It has sold over 2 million copies in the US to date. The song was also a huge success in Canada where it peaked at pole position and reached the top of the Digital Chart.

On September 28, 2008, the song entered the UK Singles Chart at number 38 on downloads alone based on two days' worth of sales. After the song's physical release the following week 'So What' knocked Kings of Leon's 'Sex On Fire' off the top slot, beating the comeback singles from Oasis ('The Shock of the Lightning') and Boyzone ('Love You Anyway'). It was Pink's second solo number one single in the UK, the first being 'Just Like a Pill', and third overall, including 'Lady Marmalade'. It also set the record for the biggest jump to number one within the Top 40, jumping 37 places to the top and, in the process, beating 2007's 34-place leap by Sugababes' 'About You Now'. In Britain 'So What' sold more copies in its first full week than any other single of 2008 apart from Duffy's 'Mercy' and Estelle's 'American Boy'. On October 19, 2008, 'So What' enjoyed its third week at the top of the UK charts. By December it was announced that 'So What' was the 14th biggest selling song of the year, with sales of around 360,000, affording it double-platinum status.

Meanwhile, Down Under, 'So What' became Pink's fourth number one in Australia. It even set an iTunes record there, debuting at number one only eight minutes after release. It also reached number one on the official New Zealand RIANZ chart, her first chart-topper there since 'Don't Let Me Get Me' in 2002 and fourth number one to date (it was the first country in which 'So What' became number one). It spent five consecutive weeks at the top in New Zealand and was certified gold after eight weeks with sales of 7,500+. After 22 weeks on the chart, it was certified platinum, selling over 15,000 copies.

In Europe, the single fared just as well. It became Pink's highest debut in Sweden, entering at number nine, eventually climbing to number two, making it her highest charting single there, in Denmark it debuted at number 14, and in Finland at number 13. It peaked at number four in the Netherlands, at number four in Belgium, and at number one in Austria and Germany.

As for the Dave Meyers video, after its release in September 2008, it jumped to the number one video spot on the iTunes chart in less than 24 hours of it being listed. It was ranked on VH1 as the third best music video on the Top 40 Videos of 2008, on Facebook it was the second favourite video of the year, while on Pink's official YouTube channel the video gained over 26 million views, making it her most viewed video on the site to date. Pink performed the single at the 2008 MTV Video

Music Awards, and it was used to promote the 2008 MTV Video Music Awards Latin America. She also sang it at the MTV Europe Music Awards 2008 that November.

The critical reception for 'So What' was just as positive. *Billboard* praised the "insatiable melodic verses meant for massive car singalongs and a chorus combustion followed by a fist-in-the-air refrain", adding that its "irresistible soundscape will transform listeners into rock stars singing their very own breakup song." *Blender* magazine commented, "The disses are a bit immature ['I'm just fine and you're a tool'] but there's a voyeuristic allure to the track." UK entertainment website Digital Spy decided it was "packed with attitude" and "terrifically catchy", awarding it 5/5 stars and later placing it as their top single of 2008. *Rolling Stone* voted it at number 29 in their list of the 100 Best Songs of 2008. *Time* magazine named it the number two song of 2008. VH1's Top 40 Videos of 2008 ranked it at number three on their list. There was one dissenting voice: The Onion's AV Club called it "so blaring and bad as to make [her next album] seem like a lost cause from the start".

It did creditably at that year's awards ceremonies as well: it was nominated at the 51st Grammy Awards for Best Female Pop Vocal Performance (alongside 'Chasing Pavements' by Adele, 'Love Song' by Sara Bareilles, 'Mercy' by Duffy, 'I Kissed A Girl' by Katy Perry and 'Bleeding Love' by Leona Lewis), and it won the award for MTV's Most Addictive Track and the MTV Video Music Award for Best Pop Video.

For Pink, the sense of euphoria was sustained by events outside the pop milieu when, in November 2008, Barack Obama became the 44th President of the United States of America, a historic occasion that prompted Pink to vow to never perform her George Bush bitch-fest 'Dear Mr. President' again. At a performance in London on the night of the US election, Pink declared her intention to sing the "battle cry" for the final time. She told the crowd: "It's Election Day. Oh God, I'm very, very nervous... We're going to win and this is the last time that I will be performing 'Dear Mr. President'.

"The next President," she continued, "is going to be an ass-kicker. The whole world is gonna change or else this will become a really fucked-up song."

That same month, conversely, Pink gave some idea of the demons with which she still wrestled and of the sense of disturbance behind the bubbly exterior. She revealed that the last Thanksgiving she spent with her family was not a success, recalling that she started drinking tequila with friends in the morning and was in no fit state to attend dinner. The six of them together consumed three bottles of Patron before 11am, and during Grace the singer took it upon herself, in her inebriated state, to dump a bowl of sweet potatoes on the head of a member of her family. "I ended up in the pool," she ranted, "and I almost had a heart attack and then I was chopping ice and I cut my hand open. I had to go to the E.R. but I couldn't feel a thing." She went on: "It was fascinating, actually — when you're that drunk and you can just watch the stitches happening." She added that she had a fit of pyromania and attended the family get-together with her ex-husband, not that these two facts were particularly connected. "I set my bedroom on fire because we [she and Hart] went upstairs to have a quickie and I left a cigarette in the oven mitt."

Around this time Pink admitted to journalist Louise Gannon that she had been to see a specialist, fearing that she was an alcoholic. "I have a problem with my vices," she confided. "I've kicked the drugs but every now and then I have to go out and get completely wasted on alcohol. For me it's all about losing control. I'm such a control freak and it's very hard for me to lose my inhibitions without something chemical inside me. "How," she wondered, "do you really have fun if there isn't a little drink in you?" She explained that she had checked into Canyon Ranch in Tucson, Arizona, in summer 2008 and had been to visit a therapist, to whom she declared that she was, indeed, an alcoholic. She proceeded to read the AA manual "from cover to cover" and they talked. Eventually, she came to the realisation that she wasn't an alcoholic, "just someone who likes to get drunk every now and then."

Also in November 2008 a TV reporter announced that she had quit her job following a disastrous interview with Pink. Hannah Hodson, it was alleged, became aggressive with the pop star while interviewing her for New Zealand's TVNZ the month before. Hodson was said to be angry that Pink had fired her sister from working as her assistant. Pink stormed out of the interview and her manager reportedly tried to confiscate the tape. The encounter was never aired on current affairs show *Close Up* after being described as a "train wreck". Pink claimed that she attempted to keep calm during the interview but found that it "was really hard to stay".

In December, Pink, talking about the many tattoos that adorned her body, decided that her favourite was the one that said, "What comes around goes around." This was because it reflected her perspective on life. She mused: "It's my only truth that never changes. I believe in karma. I believe that it comes around in both ways. I've watched really good people have really hard times and then all of a sudden something beautiful happens. I've seen instant karma and I've seen karma that I think takes lifetimes. And I've felt a lot of it."

Pink had obviously accrued a lot of good karma over the years because she was about to enjoy the greatest success of her career.

Chapter 9

Funhouse

"Love is supposed to be fun, but it can sometimes be really scary. So, too, are the funhouse mirrors that make you look so distorted that you don't recognise yourself and make you ask yourself, 'How did I get here? How do I get out of here?'"

Pink's fifth album was originally going to be titled *Punchbag*. Rumours even began circulating that she was going to call it *Heartbreak Is A Motherfucker*, but that her record label declined because of fears that such offensive language on the front cover would have a dramatic impact on sales. And yet, if relations between her and her former husband Carey Hart had been going well since the couple split, and their marriage had been the proverbial bed of roses, there remained the sense that she was still keen to project the idea of herself as emotionally damaged by the experience.

Even with its revised title of *Funhouse*, that original idea of the album as a document of a troubled affair prevailed when you saw what she'd called the songs: 'I Don't Believe You', 'One Foot Wrong', 'Please Don't Leave Me', 'Bad Influence', 'Mean', 'It's All Your Fault', 'Boring'... They all suggested that this was going to be a fairly vivid, unforgiving, autobiographical account of a failed marriage. There was even a track called 'Sober' that, at least in its title, appeared to allude to her problems with the bottle. Even the song 'This Is How It Goes Down' had about it the air of doomed finality, while bonus track 'Why Did I Ever Like You' pretty much spoke for itself.

In fact, it wasn't long after the release of *Funhouse*, at the end of October 2008, that people started talking about the album as Pink's very own *Here My Dear*, *Blood On The Tracks* or *Shoot Out The Lights*, those classic, uncompromisingly honest LP-portrayals of marriage breakdowns by, respectively, Marvin Gaye, Bob Dylan and Richard & Linda Thompson. Pink, in a press statement to accompany its release, described it as her "most vulnerable" album to date. A song by song examination of *Funhouse* bore this out, and then some. 'So What' couldn't have been a more belligerent opener, the singer announcing her intention to "start a fight" (see Chapter 8), but it hardly set the tone for what was a dolorous, downbeat, self-examining affair. 'Sober', which musically resembled 'Under The Bridge' by Red Hot Chili Peppers and would be the next track lifted off the album for single release in November 2008, was apparently written by Pink about a party that she hosted at her house where everyone was drunk or drinking except for her, a party that she wanted them all to leave. So she went to the beach and, as the sun came up, the line, "How do I feel so good sober?" came into her head. The lyrics suggested it was less about the perils of booze than it was a complaint about the pressure she was beginning to feel to be the perennial party girl and the loneliness of the long-distance pop star, being away from home and the man she loved: "I don't wanna be the girl who laughs the loudest/Or the girl who never wants to be alone," it went, and eventually it became evident that this was a song about crutches and addictions, and the many forms they take. "How do I feel so good with just me, without anyone to lean on?" wondered Pink in an interview at the time. The pared-down, almost bluesy lament, 'I Don't Believe You', painted a stark picture of the aftermath of yet another domestic brawl, when a couple come to realise there's a vast difference between fucking/fighting and love: "We come to blows/And every night/The passion's there/So it's got to be right/Right?"

'One Foot Wrong' was another gloomy number that captured Pink in a bleak mood – "All the lights are on but I'm in the dark" – wondering, "Who's gonna find me?" and being faced with the bitter truth: her other half would only be able to love her "when I'm gone" (although in a couple of reviews it was purported to be about a bad acid trip). Said Pink at the time: "That song is about losing control and how easy it is to lose the plot in life and teeter on the edge." On 'Please Don't Leave Me', over a lugubrious bassline that appeared to have wandered in from an early New Order song, a heartbroken Pink owned up to her shortcomings ("How did I become so obnoxious?"), hurling insults at her boyfriend and kicking him out of the house before acknowledging the sadistic pleasure of it all and begging him to stay: "I cannot be without you, you're my perfect little punching bag." The last two words subverted expectations: so she wasn't the punchbag of the original album title; it was Hart all along.

'Bad Influence' would presumably have closed side one in an earlier, vinyl age, and it was the first track on the album since 'So What' to be anything other than morose. Lyrically it reasserted

Pink as the party-starter, although there was an underlying sense of ennui here as she sang about winding herself up so people could watch her go. The title track maintained the upbeat pace with its funk-rock strut but the theme was more in keeping with most of "side one" with its images of Pink dancing around an empty house and the echoes of "screaming down the halls". It turned out that the titular house wasn't much fun at all; in fact it appeared to be haunted by the ghosts of a long-dead affair – so she decided to torch it, to burn it down to rid it of evil clowns. In an interview at the time, Pink spoke about how, once she and Hart split up, she only ever returned to the marital home on one occasion.

"I couldn't live there anymore," she told Louise Gannon. "I bought a house on the beach and forced myself to go in the water every day – I've always had this total terror of sharks. I had to give myself a big challenge to focus on. Then a few months later I was in a recording studio across town. It was late, I had to be back in the studio early, and it was a long drive to the beach. I thought I'd go to my old home, just to sleep. I turned up but I didn't actually have a key, so I crawled into the house through a dog flap. It felt so weird. Of course I didn't go to sleep. I went straight to the wedding-album photos and looked through them, crying and sobbing. I was there for an hour, then I just jumped up and ran out. I haven't been back since. You see, I'm not so tough."

The *Funhouse* album cover shot by Deborah Anderson, the daughter of Jon Anderson of British prog-rock group Yes, who had photographed Pink before, pursued the carnival theme, with a shot of Pink on the front having fun on a wooden horse on a fairground carousel and with a great big grin on her face that screamed, "I'm single and loving it!" It couldn't have been a bigger red herring.

Pink talked at the time about carnivals, the sinister undercurrent she detected whenever she visited them, and the way they provided a metaphor for life and love: "Clowns are supposed to be happy, but they are really scary. Carnivals are supposed to be fun, but really they are kind of creepy. And that's like life to me, and love. Love is supposed to be fun, but it can sometimes be really scary. So, too, are the funhouse mirrors that make you look so distorted that you don't recognise yourself and make you ask yourself, 'How did I get here? How do I get out of here?' But you think that you want to do it again. That is the same as love and life. It's a metaphor for being in love and for life." The track 'Funhouse', she said, was about "when the box you're in doesn't fit anymore, burn that fucker down and start a new one."

'Crystal Ball', a simple, unadorned ballad that recast Pink as an acoustic troubadour, as though she were a singer-songwriter adrift from the early-'70s counterculture era, was the track she was most proud of from 'Funhouse'. She said of it: "I recorded it in one take and we didn't mix it. It just went straight to master. It was all about a vibe and not about perfection or being polished. I just love that song and I loved recording it." Co-penned by Billy Mann, her collaborator on 'Stupid Girls', 'Dear Mr. President' and 'I'm Not Dead' among others, 'Crystal Ball' found Pink drinking wine and plagued by self-doubt. She'd been through the mill but she wouldn't swap it for anything: "Oh, I've felt that fire, and I, I've been burned/ But I wouldn't trade the pain for what I've learned." 'Mean' ("How did we get so mean?") was another bluesy rock ballad that yearned for the days when her lover used to send her flowers "even when you fucked up in my dreams." Now the sweet-nothing whispers had been replaced by screams, the passion had all but died, and the fear was that they were only together "'cause we're scared to be alone."

'It's All Your Fault' went from atmospheric mid-tempo number to explosive electro-rocker, and it caught Pink breathless, out of her mind, fearful of a future apart from her ex: "I conjure up the thought of being gone/But I'd probably even do that wrong." So she issued him an ultimatum: "I feel like we could be really awesome together/So make up your mind because it's now or never." 'Ave Mary A' drew lines between the chaos in Pink's head, the turmoil of her marriage, and a world in crisis, referencing suicide bombers, even the tragic shooting of Brazilian national, Jean Charles De Menezes, on the London Underground in 2005 in the wake of the July 7 bombings. The piano-led ballad, 'Glitter In The Air', sounded more like Tori Amos than Pink, and found her asking deep questions about fear and whether she hated herself for staring at the phone, presumably wishing it would ring. Pink admitted at the time, "I still don't have some of the answers to the questions I pose on this record. I'm still figuring it all out."

On the penultimate track 'This Is How It Goes Down' (available only on UK versions of *Funhouse*), a melodic rock-dance belter featuring a rap from Travis McCoy of hip hop-rock outfit Gym Class Heroes, Pink was in spiteful, vengeful form, having caught her lover cheating: "You will be old, homeless and broken," she spat, only half-believing her words. "Gonna crawl round on your knees/When you realise that no one's gonna measure up to me." It sounded as though the protagonist was trying to convince herself as much as she was him. Then she tormented herself, asking him questions she didn't really want him to answer ("Does she purr? Does she make it hard?"), before taunting him with what he was going to miss about her ("I'm gonna rage/Stay out really late/I'm gonna hang with all my friends you hate/I may try that threesome/Better late than never..."). Finally, 'Boring' saw Pink looking to the future, envisioning life after the love had gone (to paraphrase Earth, Wind & Fire) and all the men who were now potentially hers for the taking – if, that is, she could find one that she liked, because the track was a litany of all the things (the fast cars, the rock band entourage, the bling) that failed to get Pink, or at least her character in the song, remotely excited.

Pink had written and recorded approximately 30 to 35 songs for *Funhouse*, and they were all precious to her, to the extent that she was reluctant to let any of them go. "It's like getting rid of your children: 'I like that one, too, but I'm going to let that one die,'" she said of the distress she felt at having to pick the songs for the album and decide which wouldn't make the final cut. Luckily for her, there was the option of placing unused tracks on albums in different territories, or using them as extra tracks on singles. "The good thing now is that different countries want extra songs and B-sides, so there's always a home for the other kids." She left one of her most vicious little nippers for the iTunes version of *Funhouse*: 'Why Did I Ever Like You' easily managed to maintain the vitriolic mood, Pink raging that, even during an earthquake measuring 5.8 on the Richter scale, she'd "still have all my hate for you intact." 'Could've Had Everything', which appeared on the B-side of 'So What' as well as on the Australian iTunes (Deluxe) and US iTunes (Deluxe) versions of the album, was no barrel of laughs, either: it saw Pink backed into a corner, hated by all her friends and consumed by self-loathing for sabotaging the best thing that had ever happened to her.

Then there was 'When We're Through', pencilled in as the B-side to 'Sober', which offered a glimpse of Pink almost delusional with emotional pain, unable to tell what the weather was because she was locked in her darkened room, with "acid in my stomach", crying herself to sleep on the floor as Janis played on the stereo – the one note of self-congratulation came when she praised herself for doing what Joplin had failed to do: make it past 27, small mercy given the realisation that, "Life is just a little part of what the world will do/It brings us to the brink and beats the shit right outta you." There were several other songs written and recorded by Pink during this period, their titles – 'So Clever', 'So I', 'Leave Me Today', 'To Love Me Now', 'What Ya Want From Me?' and 'Is That The Best You've Got' – hinting at yet more anguish and invective.

Pink travelled the world to write and record the album, working with the likes of Eg White in London and Max Martin in Stockholm. Recalling the experience, she said, "It was really good to get out of my house and get away from my life. No distractions. No phones." She said the themes of the album could be summed up as, "Okay, I'm an asshole, but love me anyway." She admitted that the album's tone resulted from some of the turmoil she had been experiencing during writing and recording. "Creating songs is my favourite part, but I've had consistent agony and joy in all of the records. I'm always defensive and a survival-oriented person. I think when I'm writing songs it's my chance to be vulnerable." She added, oddly, that she didn't want *Funhouse* to come across to listeners as a break-up album:"There is a lot of that [break-up] on there, but there is fun stuff happening, too, and that's why I named it *Funhouse* in the end."

It was a surprising comment considering the by turns bitter and bolshy, angsty and aggressive nature of the project, where the shafts of light were few and far between, and mostly musical not lyrical. More startling was that, for all the allusions to breaking up and falling apart, Pink and her estranged husband never actually signed legal documents to instigate divorce proceedings even though they had been planned. But most shocking of all, after arguably one of the most rancorous records ever made in the name of mainstream pop, was that Pink and Hart would soon reunite. Maybe *Funhouse* wasn't about Pink at all and she was just playing the part of the aggrieved party. Either that or it was autobiographical and by the time it was done she had worked all of the rage out of her system...

Considering its tone of bitter unpleasantness, *Funhouse* might not have been expected to perform as well as some of her other albums, but the truth was, it fared better than any other Pink record apart from *M!ssundaztood*, and in some territories it even outstripped that career high. It reached number one on the charts in Australia, New Zealand and the UK, where it sold over 37,100 copies in its first day, ahead of Snow Patrol's *A Hundred Million Suns*. *Funhouse* became her first British number one album and was certified platinum with total sales of 684,000. On December 28, 2008, it was announced as the ninth biggest-selling record of the year, despite only being available for nine weeks out of the 52. It debuted at number two in Germany, Ireland, France and the United States (behind AC/DC's comeback album *Black Ice* in the latter territory). It has sold over 3.5 million copies worldwide. The album's lead single, 'So What', is the biggest solo success of Pink's career to date, topping the charts in 11 countries, including the US, the UK, Germany and Australia, and reaching the Top five in many others. The album also spawned hit single 'Sober' which reached the Top 20 in almost 20 countries including the US, Canada and many others, making *Funhouse* Pink's first album since *M!ssundaztood* to have its first two successive singles peak in the Top 20 of the *Billboard* Hot 100.

After weeks of falling down the *Billboard* 200, *Funhouse* rebounded from number 21 to number 13 and, by March 2009, it was certified platinum by the RIAA for selling over 1 million copies. *Funhouse* debuted at number one in the Netherlands, her highest first-week position ever there. In Switzerland, it also debuted at pole position, selling over 30,000 copies and going platinum in its first week. There was a minor furore in Australia where record shops broke embargo and placed *Funhouse* on sale one day before the release date. It still managed to be the fourth highest-selling album of the week, with only one day of sales. It sold 86,273 units that week (the highest first-week sales of 2008), and was immediately certified double-platinum. *Funhouse* eventually achieved nine consecutive weeks at the top, tying with The Beatles' compilation *1* (20 November 2000–21 January 2001). *Funhouse* was certified seven-times platinum after only three months of release. In April 2009, Pink became the only artist to have three albums in the Australian Top 50 with *Funhouse* at number eight and *M!ssundaztood* and *I'm Not Dead* charting respectively at number 32 and number 46. Something of an icon Down Under, Pink was the guest of honour at the 2008 ARIA Music Awards held in Sydney, where she performed 'So What', receiving a standing ovation from the Australian music industry. In New Zealand, *Funhouse* debuted at number one, her highest debut there, and was certified double-platinum soon after.

To promote the album and attendant debut single, Pink performed 'So What' live at the 2008 American MTV Video Music Awards. She performed various songs from her new album on British TV's 4Music in October 2008, including 'So What', 'Sober', 'Please Don't Leave Me' and her earlier UK number one hit 'Just Like A Pill'. She performed the song 'Funhouse' live on *Sunrise*, an Australian breakfast YV show, as well as playing a "Secret Gig" at The Metro in Sydney, while on her promo visit there. A *Funhouse* iPhone App was created in support of the album, making Pink the first musical artist to have a themed promotional application to be made for the iPhone App platform.

In November Pink performed 'So What' at the MTV Europe Music Awards during a live show where 40,000 feathers were released on stage, preventing her from singing the line, "And you're a tool, so..." Pink also performed 'Sober' (and, presumably, while sober) at another big award show, the 2008 American Music Awards, in November. She played a "Secret Gig" at the Cafe Du Paris in London and held another secret showcase in Barcelona, Spain. She appeared at the Bellagio Hotel in Las Vegas, Nevada, for the launch of the album in the US. She made numerous appearances on chat-shows to coincide with the album's release, including *The Today Show*, *The View*, *Late Night With Conan O'Brien*, the CBS *Early Show*, the *Ellen Degeneres Show* and *The Paul O'Grady Show* in the UK. She recorded a performance for the Divas II benefit for breast cancer in the UK but was unable to attend due to the fact that she was performing at the American Music Awards, and she performed 'Sober' on the *Australian Idol Verdict Show*.

Reviews of *Funhouse* were generally positive. Sydney's *Daily Telegraph* called it "a balanced blend of upbeat pop gems and midtempo ballads", adding that, "The power of Pink's pop lies in the clever juxtaposition of heartfelt honesty about her life with anthemic choruses and irresistible melodies tailor-made to be screamed out by her fans." *US Magazine* gave the album four stars, saying, "The rebellious Grammy winner again fuses unrestrained lyrics with perfect pop-rock hooks on her electrifying fifth CD. From her aggressive number one hit 'So What' to the vulnerable 'Please Don't Leave Me' and the open-hearted ballad 'I Don't Believe You', along with the angry 'It's All Your Fault', Pink confirms that she's still in excellent fighting shape."

Mixed reviews came from prestigious rock magazines such as *Rolling Stone* and *Blender* (although the latter has since folded), each giving the album three stars. *Rolling Stone* decided that, "Pink has shown more personality before, and some cuts, including the gloopy ballad 'I Don't Believe You', make her sound like just another big-voiced chart-buster. *Funhouse* would be more fun if Pink went easier on the bad-love songs."

In the UK, the *Guardian* drew comparisons between Pink's album and the 1970 record of the same title by punk pioneers Iggy & The Stooges: "The muscle-bound 'So What' sounds like something a female, poppy Iggy [Pop] might have created, and there's also a connection, in spirit at least, between Pink and Pop on the slow, queasy 'One Foot Wrong'. Frustratingly, the sound and the fury are followed by a string of damp ballads charting her split from her husband, but *Funhouse* is a solid album nevertheless."

Elsewhere, *Funhouse* was praised for having a "greater thematic heft than any of her previous efforts" and for its "massive, punchy hooks" that have made Pink "one of the most consistent, reliable singles artists of the last decade." One magazine hailed her "America's most soul-baring mainstream singer", and concluded: "Whether struggling with sobriety or confronting her own meanness, Pink has never been less cool: she's hot-blooded throughout, and it suits both her pipes and a female pop genre that rarely embraces this much tangible pain."

Like her previous albums, *Funhouse* contained a generous

number of hit singles. 'Sober', the second single, was described by Pink as "a dark, kind of sad song. And it's about the vices that we choose and I had this idea in my head, like, 'How do I feel this good sober?' I don't know, it's just a really, really personal, beautiful song, and it's one of my favourites." It fared well around the world, notably in America where it climbed to number one on the Adult Top 40, making it her third consecutive chart-topper following on from 'Who Knew' and 'So What' – it was the first time an artist had scored three consecutive number ones in the chart's history. It has since sold over 1 million downloads in the United States, becoming the second million-selling song from the *Funhouse* album. In the UK it rose to number nine, becoming Pink's second consecutive Top 10 hit from *Funhouse*, and her 14th Top 10 hit overall on the UK Singles Chart.

The music video for 'Sober' has been viewed over 20 million times on Youtube. Directed by Sweden's Jonas Akerlund (who worked with Madonna on the song 'Ray Of Light'), it was filmed in the last days of September in Stockholm and featured a darkly lit party scene in which Pink's doppelgänger is drunk and flirting with both boys and girls, helping her alter ego as she throws up in the bathroom, even at one point making out with herself. We always knew Pink was sexually adventurous, but this took polymorphous perversity to whole new levels.

The album's third single was 'Please Don't Leave Me', for many the best track lifted off *Funhouse* for individual release. According to *Digital Spy*, "Pink's bruised vocals – which convey the combination of bitterness and regret in her lyrics perfectly – leave the biggest impression." The video was directed by Dave Meyers, who did Pink's shorts for 'Stupid Girls', 'U + Ur Hand' and 'So What'. But this was easily his darkest, most blackly comic effort to date, including as it did references to the 1990 Stephen King-based film *Misery*, as well as other movie chillers such as *The Shining* and *What Ever Happened To Baby Jane?* The hapless male lead in the video was played by actor Eric Lively.

The story begins inside Pink's house, where after a fight with her boyfriend, she is shown trying to stop him from packing to leave. He departs the bedroom with his bags, and as he reaches the stairway Pink pleads with him to stay. He refuses and turns to go. As he does, he slips on some marbles on the floor and falls down the stairs. He sees Pink coming towards him with a pseudo-innocent expression on her face, and blacks out. When he comes to, he is bruised and swollen in bed with Pink, in something resembling a nurse's outfit, stitching up one of his wounds. She dances suggestively for him, while he tries to grasp for the telephone by the bed, only to have Pink smash his kneecaps with a golf club (a direct quote from *Misery*). Pink is then shown in the kitchen preparing a salad, angrily chopping the vegetables with a large knife. Her boyfriend wakes up in bed, and attempts to sneak out through the door, but Pink catches him at the doorway. He opens the door, only to be attacked by one of Pink's dogs. He is next shown opening his eyes to find Pink glaring at him once again. She paints his face with clown's makeup while he sits uncomfortably in a wheelchair. His hands are tied, and his face is battered and bruised. Pink grabs his wheelchair, spins it around and pushes it off a high step, smiling as she does so. He flies out of the chair, into a room filled with objects seemingly from a carnival such as merry-go-round horses and various dolls. He attempts another escape but Pink chases him into the garage, where she grabs an axe and stalks him through the house. He reaches the upstairs bathroom, and shuts the door just in time to block Pink charging psychotically down the hallway with the axe. The axe smashes through the door, leaving a hole for Pink to peer through with a menacingly benign expression, another direct nod, this time to the Stephen King-based film *The Shining*. The man grabs a spray-can and sprays her eyes. Blinded, she flails backwards, and slips on the same marbles as before, and she falls over the upstairs railing. The final scene shows the paramedics taking the man out on a stretcher, and Pink sprawled on the floor with her leg broken and the axe beside her.

Hardly surprisingly given the violent scenes and disturbing imagery, there were two versions cut of the video – one of them had to be a censored version, minus many of the scenes of sadistic pleasure. In the latter version, Pink's boyfriend isn't shown falling down the stairs, when he is in bed the sewn stitches on his arm are not seen, the scene of Pink smashing his leg with the golf club is removed, the angry vegetable-chopping scene is shorter, a lot of the boyfriend's bloody cuts are not visible and the dog isn't shown attacking him. Also cut was the scene where Pink punches his arm, and she isn't shown holding the axe as she chases him. In the bathroom scene, Pink chopping a hole in the door with the axe is cut and we don't see her sprayed with the aerosol, although we do still get to see her doing her best Jack Nicholson impression: "Heeere's Pink!"

The full, uncensored version of the video first aired on UK television on 4Music in March 2009, but understandably it was given a late-night showing, on the back of which the single peaked at number 12, making it her 17th Top 20 British hit. On the Official Australian Airplay chart, the song debuted at number eight, the highest first-week position ever on this chart after Delta Goodrem's 'In This Life' which debuted at number six in September 2007. In its third week on the

Airplay Chart it peaked at number one, Pink's third consecutive single to do so. In the United States, 'Please Don't Leave Me' reached number 20, Pink's third Top 20 entry from *Funhouse*, as well as her sixth consecutive Top 20 entry on the *Billboard* Hot 100 chart.

'Bad Influence' was the unofficial fourth single in Australia and New Zealand: it was released to radio in April 2009 and there was a physical release mooted for May to coincide with Pink's Australian tour. At the time of writing this book it was already in the Top 10 of the Australian iTunes chart and was receiving heavy airplay in Australia and New Zealand, where it quickly became a radio hit and as usual reached number one on the Australian Airplay Chart. It spent two weeks at number one then fell before, on June 6, reclaiming the top slot after Pink's Australian tour sparked radio coverage. In New Zealand, 'Bad Influence' debuted at number 33 on May 18, 2009, jumping to number 27 the following week. It has so far peaked at number 14. However, no official announcement about the song being a single Down Under had been made, and no music video had been confirmed.

Also at the time of writing the book, the title track of *Funhouse* was announced as the fourth UK single, with an anticipated release of August 24, 2009. Her record label, SonyBMG, described the accompanying short as "one of the most fun times Pink has ever had making a video – it's so her and the fans will not be disappointed at this masterpiece." According to insiders, the video is "mysterious", with numerous "twists and turns along the way" as well as special effects, including the blowing up of a house. "This video," they predicted, "will go down in Pink's history."

Apparently, Pink hadn't quite got Carey Hart out of her system...

Chapter 10

This Is How It Goes Down

"Anger is the most necessary emotion. It is a survival instinct and we're meant to feel it – a fight or flight kind of deal. If expressed in the right way, anger is the most healthy feeling you can have."

AFTER the Party Tour of 2002, the 2004 Try This Tour and the I'm Not Dead Tour, which was one of the most successful tours of 2006-7, came the Funhouse Tour, the fourth such live global foray undertaken by Pink in her decade-long career. Taking her 2000 debut album *Can't Take Me Home* as the starting point, it marked 10 full years at the top for the world's leading purveyor of angsty rock, pop, disco and lite metal. Coincidentally, that other troubled former teen-pop starlet, Britney Spears, announced her own Circus Tour, on the back of her December 2008 album *Circus*, just after Pink declared her intention to fill the world's stadia with carnivalesque glory.

"Had I known that certain other people were going to base their latest tour on circus stuff, I probably would have gone in another direction," Pink said, pointing out that she had the idea first: "I was six months before that. And I didn't really understand that it was a trend that was happening. I'm pretty out of the loop."

Not that anyone would be able to confuse the tours, she said, comparing and contrasting Spears' lip-synched, dance-oriented spectacular and Pink's gritty, emotional rock 'n' roll affair, which she promised would be like "two hours of group therapy." Elaborating on the "circus" theme, she claimed that circuses were good because they were "full of what mainstream society considers freakish; the outcasts." She also decided the theme was "kind of sexy and exciting and big and over the top."

The ticket sales for the Funhouse Tour were pretty big and over the top. The tour was announced on October 14, 2008, nearly two weeks before the release of her fifth studio album. Pink stated, "I'm so excited to get back on the road. The Funhouse Tour ideas are running rampant in my head. Who knows what they'll come out as... And I can't wait to see." After a long discussion as to whether Pink was going to perform in her home country, it was officially announced on April 2, 2009, that the tour would start in Seattle and end in Hannover, Germany at the TUI Arena. Demand for tickets in Australia was particular high: Pink broke her own record when she sold out seven consecutive shows in Sydney in 40 minutes. The overwhelming desire to see Pink live in Australia meant that she surpassed her record-breaking run of 35 sold-out shows achieved on the 2007 Australian leg of the I'm Not

Dead Tour, which grossed $41 million. The Funhouse Tour would comprise an astonishing 58 shows in one of her favourite territories.

Pink announced 17 dates alone at the Rod Laver Arena in Melbourne, thereby breaking Australian John Farnham's record for most concerts at the venue in one tour; it also meant that almost five per cent of the Melbourne population would eventually have seen Pink live on the Funhouse tour. She would also perform 10 shows at the Sydney Entertainment Centre and 12 in Sydney altogether; by the end of her sojourn in Sydney 115,598 people would have seen the show, making Pink the most successful touring artist in the city after Kylie Minogue (appropriately enough, a DVD of the tour was filmed at the June 6, 2009, show in Sydney). Over 600,000 tickets were sold in Australia at the time of writing, with estimates suggesting Pink would earn between $56 and $70 million from the Australian leg of the Funhouse Tour. Overall ticket sales around the world were believed to have been in excess of 2 million.

The opening acts on some of Pink's European dates included a new British band signed to Sony/BMG called Raygun, Faker who were chosen for the Australian leg of her tour, and The Ting Tings who supported Pink at some of her US shows. The shows were broken into several sections: 'Intro' (a.k.a. 'Highway To Hell'); 'Rockstar' (including such songs as 'Bad Influence', 'Just Like A Pill' and 'Who Knew'); a section called 'Seduce & Love' during which she sang the likes of 'Please Don't Leave Me', 'U + Ur Hand', 'Leave Me Alone (I'm Lonely)' and 'So What'; a 'Piano/Acoustic' interlude (for songs such as 'Family Portrait', 'I Don't Believe You', 'Crystal Ball', 'Trouble' and a version of the traditional folk tune 'Babe I'm Gonna Leave You', famously covered by Led Zeppelin on their début album); a segment called 'Welcome To The Funhouse' ('Sober', 'Funhouse', 'Crazy' and a hysterical rendition of Queen's 'Bohemian Rhapsody' for which, in London at least, she wore a cartoonish yachting cap and yellow frock-coat); and finally the 'Encore' section, which usually comprised 'Get The Party Started' and 'Glitter In The Air'.

It wasn't quite as rigid as that sounds, and the set-list did change for some of the shows – for example, in Antwerp 'It's All Your Fault' was replaced by 'Don't Let Me Get Me'. In Dublin, Pink stopped 'I Don't Believe You' mid-song as she forgot the lyrics, and then she continued from the chorus until stopping again, saying she "didn't want to do the song any more", opting instead for Bob Marley's 'Redemption Song'. On other nights, in different cities, she also fluffed the lyrics to 'Crystal Ball' and 'I Don't Believe You' – in London on May 2, strangely, she stopped and started the latter after every verse, telling the crowd the song was "stalkerish" and taking six minutes to finish it.

There were irregularities with regard to some of her onstage exploits as well. She was meant to perform a high-flying bungee stunt every night during 'Get The Party Started' but didn't at some of the concerts in April 2009. In Brisbane, Australia, at the start of June, while Pink was singing 'Get The Party Started' her bungee wire safety-line snapped, leaving her stranded in mid-air, just hanging there for about a minute until a silk "rope" could be dropped from the roof of the Boondall Entertainment Centre. She unhooked her harness and slid down to safety. After the concert, Pink, unbowed, posted an update on her Twitter.com blog, writing, "Tonight's show was awesome! Audience was great – even when the bungees broke and I had to do the emergency silk climb :) That was so scary!!!"

Pink posted another blog after her Glasgow shows, describing them as the loudest, most ecstatic crowd noise-wise of the tour so far. And the critics were just as ecstatic. "A Pink show is more than just a pop concert – it's a major spectacle that you can't take your eyes off. The show was simply mesmerising," gushed the *Aberdeen Evening Express*. The Scottish press rather warmed to Pink during the Funhouse Tour: "Pink can rock it, that's for sure. She has the anthems, the voice and the sass," decided *The Glasgow Herald*, who awarded the show four stars. Over in Ireland, the *Independent* wrote, "She's no slouch as an aerial dare-devil, but here's one rock star at her most compelling when she has two feet planted squarely on the ground" while the *Express & Star* said, "Her singing was perfect, even when she was suspended mid-air, on her back and spinning rapidly on her harness."

The Germans, too, were impressed by Pink's ability to hold a note even while suspended in mid-air: "Headfirst she gets lifted towards the ceiling, flies over the audience, and the American sings with a quality that some of her colleagues wouldn't be able to hold, even when they were just standing," wrote the reviewer for the *Rheinische Post*. An online writer in Melbourne reported on the "concert spectacle" that saw, among other things, Pink hanging from a trapeze, getting dipped in water and sliding down a giant slide, all without the singer missing a single note. "A Pink show is always a spectacle," the reporter went on, praising the use of massive video screens, backing dancers and a cool second stage for the intimate acoustic set that occurred mid-show. "With 17 concerts sold out in Melbourne," he concluded, "as well as heaps booked for the rest of Australia, it's easy to see why she is so loved in this country."

Pink was as knocked out by the response to her Funhouse

Tour gigs as the audience were by her. As the singer looked out at the 20,000 rapturous fans at the giant O2 auditorium in London during an impressive three-night run there in May 2009, she gasped, "Holy shit" – it was almost as though, up until that point, despite almost 30 million record sales, Pink didn't quite realise how popular she was, nor that her appeal was quite so diverse. "There are," reported Caroline Sullivan of the *Guardian*, "female couples, groups of lads, tweens with parents – and many are wearing tutus like the one she sports on the cover of her most recent album, *Funhouse*, which is the kind of love that money can't buy." Watching Pink dance and shake her short bleached mop, Sullivan predicted that, "Britney and Beyoncé, due at the same venue in the next few weeks, will be less spontaneous, and a good deal less charming." The reviewer went on to commend Pink's emphasis on rock rather than pop, reserving special mention for her guitarist Spankster, whose "hairy presence imparts a gritty edge". Rock, decided Sullivan, "suits her big voice and tattooed, tomboyish style", but she also noted her theatrical, showgirl side: each song had its own visual theme, such as the disembodied hands that appeared from a chaise longue to fondle the singer during 'I Touch Myself', the mock pillow fight during 'So What' and the graceful backflips during 'Sober'. "What a terrific show," concluded the British newspaper, quite taken aback. "Who would have thought it?"

And who would have thought, while the Funhouse Tour was underway, after all the fuss and furore – not to mention the fury of the *Funhouse* album itself – that Pink and Carey Hart would ever get back together. But this did indeed appear to be on the cards by the start of 2009. It had already been confirmed that Pink and Hart were never actually divorced; now news stories began to emerge that the pair were to both travel to Australia where Carey was hosting several three-hour motocross stunt events in Sydney, Melbourne, Brisbane and Newcastle, tying in perfectly with Pink's numerous Australian dates in May.

"We are definitely back together," Pink told the *Daily Telegraph*, joking that, "We never really legally got divorced – paperwork for us is really annoying." Her estranged husband said of their joint trip Down Under, "This was one of the first steps – we had to come up with a way to be able to both go to work and both see each other. It's going to be a very exciting time for both of us to go to Australia and tour together for four months."

The reunion had looked like a distinct possibility since the start of the year – literally, since, on December 31, 2008, Hart and Pink had been seen together at the former stunt rider's Las Vegas club, where he was seen escorting her to the stage and toasting her at midnight before wishing everyone a happy new year. Pink proceeded to follow the toast with a live performance at Hard Rock Hotel's Wasted Space. Before her 30-minute performance on the club's stage, she and her ex had been hanging out in the VIP area with friends. It was reported that "they didn't really talk much, but at midnight Carey grabbed her and took her up to the stage and introduced her. He sort of led her to the stage." After the brief set, Pink went back to the VIP area and hung out with friends before leaving the club at around 2am.

The previous October, Pink had revealed that she remained "best friends" with Hart despite their break-up. Now, in 2009, she was saying that she had "no hard feelings" towards her ex-husband. Not only did the two ring in 2009 together, but they were seen variously riding a motorcycle, hiking and jogging together in Los Angeles. "The couple gazed at each other and walked arm-in-arm after their workout, before breaking into a play fight," reported one local gossip-sheet.

The pop-rocker, a tad flippantly, later admitted that she wanted to stay involved in Hart's life, even if that meant "giving him away at his next wedding". Pink did, however, quit wise-cracking long enough to acknowledge the tough side of splitting up. "It's up and down," she said. "You have strong moments and you have weak moments. But it's not just been devastating – it's been freedom, too." Pink, who revealed that she had had a belligerent streak since childhood, described her aggressive anthems such as 'So What' as part of a cathartic process that left her with mixed feelings. "It feels very confusing," she said. "It's bittersweet. It's funny, it's empowering, it's 'screw you!'... It's all of that." She also revealed that she had to attend anger management classes to deal with her issues after her marriage fell apart. She said, "Anger is the most necessary emotion. I took a class called Demystifying Anger a couple of months ago. I learned so much. That anger is a survival instinct and we're meant to feel it – a fight or flight kind of deal. If expressed in the right way, anger is the most healthy feeling you can have."

With their on-off relationship, one magazine declared that Pink and Hart were "the new Pammy and Tommy", only minus the sex tape and giant balloon breasts. According to *Us Weekly*, Hart had now moved into Pink's Malibu home. A source told the magazine, "Pink is head over heels for Carey and wants to try it again, but she is proceeding cautiously... It never really ended. They just took a break on the marriage because they couldn't make it work never seeing each other. She never gave up hope that it would work." Which is probably why, ventured the magazine a tad cynically, Pink wrote 'So What' in the interim, "a song about what a huge loser Hart is and how much better off she is without him."

In February 2009, Hart appeared to be doing everything right to ingratiate himself with Pink, even to the extent of teaming up with People for the Ethical Treatment of Animals (PETA) and fronting the organisation's new anti-fur ad campaign. In the ad, which had been unveiled at Hart's Wasted Space club in Las Vegas, the motocross racer was seen baring his tattooed chest for the camera. Striking a pose in front of a motorbike, Carey wore a red cap and had both hands crossed in front of his body. His name was inked under a tagline that read, "Ink, Not Mink". In an interview with PETA, Carey explained that his ex-wife had been encouraging him to get involved in the animal rights cause.

There was more PETA action from the pair that month when Pink teamed up with British comedian Ricky Gervais to lend their voices to a new anti-fur ad campaign dubbed "Stolen for Fashion". In the 30-second TV spot, Pink provided the voice for an alligator without its skin, while Gervais voiced a rabbit without its coat. Pink was seen unveiling the ad during Paris Fashion Week alongside her pal, Stella McCartney, a designer known for not using animal products for her fashion lines.

It was at a Stella McCartney fashion show around this time that superstar rapper Kanye West incurred Pink's anti-animal-fur wrath. She, Stella, her ex-Beatle father Paul (also vehemently anti-animal cruelty) and the Vice President of PETA were all at the show when West began gabbling on about the prospect of integrating fur into the collection. Not one to hold her tongue, Pink later spat that "Kanye West is the person pissing me off right now. The entire time Kanye is going, 'They need more fur in this show'. He just wouldn't shut up about how he loved fur. I mean, he's saying this to me, the PETA guy and Paul McCartney! I was just so grossed out by him. I'm like, 'You're an idiot!' There are so many people who I think are a waste of skin and he's up there. I should wear him." She wondered what had possessed the rapper to make such bold, unfashionable assertions in the first place, although she had an idea. "There is no way that he didn't know what he was doing," she said. "He must have been trying to get a rise of out everyone – or he was being the alpha-male superstar who was so caught up in impressing people with his knowledge of fur that he simply forgot who he was talking to. Hey, he *is* that self-absorbed."

Back in the Pink-Hart love bubble, in March 2009 Hart revealed in an interview for *SpeedFreaks* that he and Pink were now "dating" and attempting to work things out: "Sometimes," he said, "you have to take a couple of steps back to move forward." He explained in an interview for Australian radio that the couple had been forced to "grow up" to save their marriage, and that both parties only learned how to be together during the separation. "We both had a lot of growing up to do over the course of the last year. No relationship's perfect. We were apart for about a year and we started putting things back together and this is a big part of the putting back together process." He also expressed his admiration for Pink's "talent and dedication" throughout her career, even as he switched career himself, from motocross rider to something called "short core truck racing", which is apparently "like super cross in race trucks".

"The thing about Pink is she's so dedicated to her fans and to putting on amazing live shows," he said, adding that, although "she might not see the record success of a Britney

Spears", nevertheless "the girl sells a hell of a lot of albums. She's incredible."

Things took a turn for the serious in April 2009, commitment-wise, when it was announced that Pink and Hart were considering renewing their wedding vows. A close friend of Carey confirmed the news, saying in a statement, "They are very happy and spending a lot of time together." They originally broke up, the friend said, "because of their busy careers, but they never stopped loving each other...They've always had a bond, but they needed time apart to realise that they wanted to continue their marriage. They've always had a huge amount of love and respect for one another." That'll explain the golf club crashing down onto the boyfriend's leg in the 'Please Don't Leave Me' video, then. Meanwhile, a ceremony was mooted to be held at the couple's "house in Malibu on the beach at sunset", said a source. "It will take place in early summer and will be very simple and small, with just their family and a few close friends."

In an interview circa her initial split with Hart in February 2008, Pink had said of her marriage, "Nothing went wrong. I want him to be the father of my children one day, but I'm just not ready for one day yet. I want to go on dates, to be a young girl." Now, three years on, she was discussing the prospect of a second marriage to Hart. She seemed a bit perplexed herself. "I don't know where the remarriage thing came from," she said. "That kind of came out of the air. But we are definitely back together."

Talking about the couple's time apart, she said airily and grandly: "We try to protect ourselves from being fully in love and fully open and fully vulnerable, and really all we're doing is protecting ourselves from love and real love and the opportunity to really learn and grow with another person, so it's actually really detrimental, and you think it's helping. My advice would be to dive in. Absolutely, it's not going to kill you."

On the subject of their proposed remarriage, she said, "We never really legally got divorced. So we're choosing to be together." She added that their new role models were cool Hollywood actor-couples Tim Robbins and Susan Sarandon and Kurt Russell and Goldie Hawn — "People," she said, "who just choose to be together every day because they want to be there. And labels have never been our thing, so we're just diving into that empty swimming pool, headfirst."

When asked about *Funhouse* and the vitriolic nature of many of its songs, rather than shirk the question or bluff that she had exorcised all of her negative emotions, she was honest enough to admit: "I still have anger. It's really easy to just be right back there. I don't have a hard time transplanting myself straight back to that moment."

Then again, Pink being Pink, anything was possible, and even as preparations were going on behind the scenes for a purported second marriage ceremony, she was being brazen and candid in the British press about her bisexuality. "I'm not embarrassed about being bisexual. This is who I am," she said. "Love is pure and I try to keep it that way. This is who I am, what I feel. I think it's unnecessary to draw the subject out, but I think it even more stupid not to discuss it." She added, "It seems as if bisexuality is a trend and I should whip up the masses. Well, I don't believe in trends, I just believe in me."

Most controversial of all – and one can only imagine what Carey Hart would have made of this – was when she said of her renewed relationship with her formerly estranged biker husband, "I would also be just as happy with a new woman. I'm not complicated, I sing about love in all its shapes, forms and colours. I speak my mind. I sing about everyday stuff such as homosexuality and sadly the homophobia that always comes with it." Fearless as ever, she said she was unconcerned about any backlash that may accompany such bold declarations. But she also denied rumours that she had been having a special relationship with a woman. "I'm not gay," she said, confusingly, "so I guess I would not try a relationship with a woman." Besides, apart from anything else, she explained, "I like penis."

Gay, straight, bi – Pink was all of these and more, and seemingly all at once. She even got to snog notorious androgynous British comedian Russell Brand, all in the line of work, naturally. It was for a forthcoming movie called *Get Him To The Greek*, a follow-up to Brand's 2008 hit *Forgetting Sarah Marshall*. The film included kissing scenes with Christina Aguilera, with new teen-pop sensation Katy Perry (of 'I Kissed A Girl' 2008 hit single fame), and with Pink. "In the scene with Pink and Katy Perry I had to do kissing," explained the funny-man. "I got to snog them both in a day. Katy Perry is lovely. She is the kind of girl who would skip downstairs lightly. Christina was amazing. She is unbelievable – a perfect object. How could you ever talk to her about anything other than sex?" As for Pink, said Brand, "She is a lovely woman – a forceful, sexy woman."

There was no doubt about her forceful sexiness, but there was also no denying that Pink in 2009 was behaving as contrarily as ever. Confused? Split personality? Mad? Of course, there was always the possibility that she was just a bit, well, eccentric. This was, after all, the woman who, in June 2009, announced that she wanted to let one of her beloved dogs, a bulldog, fly a private jet. "I got to let my bulldog fly a private jet," she said, revealing that she once let him sit at the controls during a flight. She obviously has issues with long-distance travel because apparently, after once chartering a yacht through the Mediterranean, she considered suicide by jumping off the boat. Why? "Because I wasn't getting along with the captain," she explained. "We were out in the ocean riding the waves. I got sick and couldn't take it. So I got my favourite dress in one hand, a bottle of wine in the other and I was ready to jump in the ocean and die. Luckily Carey [Hart] talked me down."

There was obviously lunacy afoot on Planet Pink in summer 2009 because that same month an over-zealous fan reportedly breached security to gain access to the star's suite at the exclusive Palazzo Versace in Queensland where she was staying with Carey Hart during her tour of Australia. Pink was horrified to discover a fan had found her private condo and had pushed a note under the door, begging to meet the pop star on the weekend. As a result the singer checked out of the hotel early, to find a new, more secure hotel in the city.

Pink was almost as horrified by the version of her hit single 'So What' that the finalists on US TV's *American Idol* performed during the show's finale. The Top 13 *Idol* finalists delivered their rendition of the song in the results show of the singing competition on May 20, the eight boys and five girls taking the stage in all-white outfits for the performance. As she exclaimed on her Twitter page: "I heard it thru the grapevine that someone butchered my song last night on TV... does that mean I've 'made it?' lol," she wrote.

It was an opinionated summer for Pink, but then, there hadn't really been a time when she'd been exactly circumspect, unforthcoming or shy, a function, perhaps, of her celebrity lifestyle. Or maybe she just couldn't help being herself: loud, brash, impulsive, with a simultaneous propensity for both narcissism and nihilism. In an interview with Q magazine a couple of years before, she had talked about her dogs, one which she'd called Wanker. Was it embarrassing, the journalist wondered, when she had to call out Wanker's name in a crowded thoroughfare or on a busy beach?

"Fuck, no," she said, genuinely surprised at the idea. "For everyone else probably. I used to do it purposely when I lived on Venice Beach, like let him go for 400 yards and then shout, 'Wanker!', and this cute little Jack Russell would come running. I don't like people that much – that's why I have dogs. I have a warped sense of how things really are because I've been out of real life for so long."

Pink admitted that her life was somewhat less than real. And lonely, despite the fame and acclaim and the adoration of millions of fans.

"I don't know how people think I could be surrounded by a thousand people and I'd still be lonely," she said. "It's the human condition. I'm not saying it's always a bad thing; it gives me something to write about. I'm happy being miserable. Fuck it!"

She went on to talk about her drinking habits, and how she wasn't "a vomiter" when she got drunk. "I just spin out and have to go to bed – in fact, in my dream last night the room was spinning," she said. "Maybe it's because I went to bed drunk."

The journalist asked who she would call if she had a serious problem and she replied: "I have five or six great friends. I can speak to my mom now if I get into shit, but I'd probably call my dad. I was talking to him, like, 'Dad, you're 58, I'm 24. Do you ever figure all this shit out? How do you know that you're content?' He said, 'Honey, you don't. Life is a journey, not a destination.' I'm like, 'Fuck! I do all this stuff and I don't feel good about any of it.'

"All the shit I've done," she went on. "I do feel good about some things, but when things happen to you, you're just like, 'That was anti-climatic.' I always feel like I'm having an out-of-body experience, just sitting back watching."

She talked about what constituted her idea of a good time. "Maybe stay at home and watch a movie. Go to dinner, go dancing, go shoot some guns..."

Finally, she admitted that, of her many foibles, one of them was a lack of confidence, and the other was being outspoken. Talk about schizoid tendencies...

"I was always insecure but I was also very opinionated," she said. "You know, balls to the wall, full speed ahead! My thing was to prove people wrong, and that brought me to some great opportunities. But everything I say and do is seriously what I believe. I know I'm a lot to take, and I know that better than anyone. But you know what? Set me on fire, string me up, but I'm not going to shut up and I'm not going to sit down either."

Chapter 11

Good Old Days

"I no longer feel like the underdog with a point to prove."

Pink ended the noughties as she began them: as one of the biggest stars on the planet. Indeed, *Billboard*, at the end of 2009, named her the number one pop musician of the decade. Then again, bearing in mind her 18 Top 20 hits on the *Billboard* charts, including three number ones, not forgetting the 50 million albums and 80 million singles she had shifted worldwide and the three million tickets she had sold for her 2009-10 world tour, this was hardly a surprising placing.

It was also not surprising that Pink ended the decade by reflecting on her achievements, via the release, in May 2009, of a four-CD set of her albums *Can't Take Me Home*, *Missundaztood*, *Try This* and *I'm Not Dead* (excluding her then-current album *Funhouse*). Well, perhaps a little surprising. The singer had never been a fan of the backwards glance. When, 18 months later, her record company decided to issue a

145

compilation entitled *Greatest Hits… So Far!!!*, Pink responded by saying that she "was not inspired at all for this album… I always figured you need to be 60 or better, to have a little more past, to put one of these out. I fought it for years." Nevertheless, the box set fared quite well at the "box office", peaking at number seven in the UK album chart and number 13 in Australia.

Pink was such a big star in Australia that, for an October 2009 episode of *Australian Idol*, her music was the theme of the show. The rest of 2009 was taken up with the singer appearing in a documentary movie called *The People Speak* and performing her track 'Sober' at the MTV Video Music Awards – where she was nominated for Best Female Video, for 'So What' – while doing a trapeze act. Eventually, she lost out to Taylor Swift, but then, so did the other nominees: Lady Gaga, Beyoncé, Katy Perry and Kelly Clarkson, an impressive lineup by any measure.

There was more high-wire action in January 2010 at the Grammy Awards, where Pink performed 'Glitter In The Air', the fifth song to be lifted from *Funhouse* for single release and soon to be its fifth charting single, which made it her most successful album in terms of number of hits yielded. Once again she was up against Katy Perry, Taylor Swift and Beyoncé (as well as a fast-rising singer called Adele), but it was Beyoncé who won the award for Best Female Pop Vocal Performance, for 'Halo'.

The year 2010 saw Pink take part in the remake of famous eighties charity single 'We Are The World', in aid of the victims of the Haiti earthquake catastrophe that befell the country in January. She sang alongside some of the world's biggest stars, including Justin Bieber, Janet Jackson and Kanye West. There was more eighties revisiting when she sang a version of Peter Gabriel's 'Don't Give Up' with soul supremo John Legend for a multinational, cross-cultural affair, organised by jazz legend Herbie Hancock, entitled The Imagine Project. Pink was evidently in collaborative mood because in June she made a cameo appearance on a track called 'Won't Back Down' on Eminem's album *Recovery*. Eminem invited Pink to sing on the album because he "felt like she would smash this record." Produced by DJ Khalil, it was a fierce and full-on number, the website Idolator praising this "loud, angry, rockin' tune, full of energy in every single beat" and singling out Pink's "soulful (but still hard) vocals during the chorus".

Autumn 2010 saw the release of a brand new Pink track, the first single to be taken from *Greatest Hits... So Far!!!* It was called 'Raise Your Glass' and was announced by Pink via her Twitter account, mirroring the use of social media by Lady Gaga. Lyrically, the song had much in common with Gaga and the identification of herself and her fans as society's outsiders and suggested Pink had been paying close attention to the new upstart of cyber pop-disco. 'Raise Your Glass', explained Pink, was dedicated to those who "felt they were not a part of the popular crowd", the reference in the chorus to "all my under-dogs... and nitty-gritty, dirty little freaks" recalling Gaga's own coterie of "little monsters". Where Pink didn't seem to have been swayed by Gaga was in the musical direction of 'Raise Your Glass' – written by Pink, her frequent collaborator Max Martin and fellow Swedish songwriter/producer Karl Johan Schuster a.k.a. Shellback (co-writer with Pink and Martin of 'So What', and, more recently, of Taylor Swift's massive 2012 hit 'We Are Never Ever Getting Back Together'), it was firmly in the pop-rock camp, with a hefty stomp factor, fist-punching chorus and feisty attitude to match.

The video, her 12th collaboration with director Dave Meyers, also promoted inclusiveness, Gaga style, with its images of unconventional-looking females and depiction of a gay mar-riage. There was additional reference to the importance of equal rights across the sexes, races, even species, with scenes featuring Pink obstructing a matador from a bull and the singer in full Animal Liberation Front regalia, balaclava and all.

Her second single of the year (after 'Glitter In The Air', which charted at number 18 in the US in February), 'Raise Your Glass' was a success all over the world on its release in October. Although it only reached number 13 in the UK, it was number one in Australia, the Czech Republic and Hungary. It also became her tenth Top 10 hit in the US, putting her behind only Rihanna and Beyoncé in the most-top-10-hits-in-the-noughties stakes, and only her second single to peak at pole position there, following on from 'So What' – her third if you include 'Lady Marmalade', her 2001 team-up with Mya, Missy Elliot, Lil' Kim and Christina Aguilera. For Max Martin, it marked his ninth number one, having visited the spot previously with Britney Spears ('… Baby One More Time'), Katy Perry ('I Kissed A Girl') and Kelly Clarkson ('My Life Would Suck Without You'), among others. To date, it has sold four million copies globally.

Reviewers were impressed by Pink's first brand new work of the new decade, praising it for its anthemic catchiness, and deciding that it had just the right spirit of surging positivity to soundtrack a million real life parties and events. A sure sign of its infiltration of the culture came in March 2011 when the song was performed on the US TV series *Glee* and by all remaining contestants on one of the results shows of *American Idol*.

Pink had barely allowed 'Raise Your Glass' to leave the charts when she decided it was time to issue her next single, also from *Greatest Hits… So Far!!!*. In December 2010, 'Fuckin' Perfect' became her 27th single, and from its title to the lyrical content and attendant video it was clear Pink had no intention of mellowing, despite turning 30 the previous year. Another Pink-

Martin-Shellback composition – a sort of hard rock ballad – it was almost a companion piece to 'Raise Your Glass', being a song about being true to yourself and not allowing critical people or any critical voices in your head to lower your self-esteem. The chorus was a howl of reassurance and defiance seemingly directed as much at herself as at the sort of "dirty little freaks" who Pink, playing the motivational speaker, imagined peopled her following.

The video was as controversial as the song's title. Another collaboration with Dave Meyers, it was a disturbing study of abuse, depression, self-harming and suicide. It opened with a fairly graphic sex scene starring Pink – who was pregnant at the time with her first child – and went on to feature further, no less arresting scenes of a young woman (played by actress Tina Majorino) variously daubing the phrase "Skinny Bitches" in a toilet cubicle and snorting drugs as she gazes enviously at other girls, getting caught stealing a dress from a shop, weighing herself on a bathroom scale, the very picture of anorexia, and cutting the word "perfect" into her arm with a razor blade while sat in the bath.

Writing about the video on her official website, Pink said: "Cutting, and suicide, two very different symptoms of the same problem, are gaining on us (The problem being: alienation and depression. The symptoms: cutting and suicide). I personally don't know a single person who doesn't know at least two of these victims personally."

She explained that the video, provocative and shocking as it was, was designed to alert people to these issues, adding that the making of the video was a "very emotional experience", not least because of her unborn child. "I have a life inside of me, and I want her or him to know that I will accept him or her with open and loving and welcoming arms," she wrote. "And though

I will prepare this little munchkin for a sometimes cruel world,
I will also equip this kid to see all the beauty in it as well."

Pointedly, the video had a happy ending as the female protagonist was shown as a successful artist with a loving partner
and a happily sleeping baby daughter. The song itself had its
own happy afterlife, in its cleaned-up form and with its censored title, reaching number two in the States and performing
well around the world. Sadly, it lost out to Lady Gaga's 'Born
This Way' in the bid to become the 1,000th number one song
in the 52-year history of the *Billboard* chart, although it did
reach the top of both the Pop Songs and Adult Pop Songs
charts, giving Pink the record for most number ones on both.
She also made history in March 2011 when the single became
one of three songs in the top 10 to feature the "f" word – the
others were 'Fuck You' by Cee Lo Green and Enrique Iglesias'
'Tonight (I'm Fuckin' You)'. It was the first time such an event
had occurred. In November 2011, 'Fuckin' Perfect' received a
Grammy nomination for Best Pop Solo Performance and by
2012 it had sold almost three million copies.

The previous November, 2010, *Greatest Hits… So Far!!!*
became Pink's last ever album for Jive, a subsidiary of RCA –
with its disbanding, she would continue to record for the parent label. It drew on all of her albums from *Missundaztood* to
Funhouse, and included 'Raise Your Glass', 'Fuckin' Perfect' and
a track called 'Heartbreak Down' on some versions of the collection (there were slightly different track listings for different
territories). *Greatest Hits… So Far!!!* featured 16 tracks and 60
minutes of music that went some way towards establishing
Pink as the premier American female pop-rock singles act of
her era. It debuted at number 14 in the States and peaked at
number five, the exact same position it climbed to in the UK,
while in Australia and New Zealand it reached number one.

Pink in the hoop, channelling her inner Napoleon at the Palais De Nikaia in Nice, on February 24, 2009.

Glammed up for the 52nd Annual Grammy Awards at the Staples Center in Los Angeles on January 31, 2010, Pink performed 'Glitter In The Air' before posing in the press room. (STEVE GRANITZ/WIREIMAGE)

Pink becomes the newest face of Covergirl Cosmetics at Shutters On The Beach in Santa Monica, California, August 6, 2012. (ANGELA WEISS/GETTY IMAGES)

Pink and Carey Hart arrive at the 2012 MTV Video Music Awards at Staples Center in LA on September 6, 2012. (STEVE GRANITZ/WIREIMAGE)

Pink, Carey Hart and Willow Hart in Tribeca, New York, September 17, 2012. (ALO CEBALLOS/FILMMAGIC)

Pink in the SiriusXM studio in New York, July 9, 2012. (CINDY ORD/GETTY IMAGES)

Guitarist Tom Dumont, Gwen Stefani of No Doubt and Pink onstage during the 2012 iHeartRadio Music Festival at the MGM Grand Garden Arena, Las Vegas, September 21, 2012. (CHRISTOPHER POLK/GETTY IMAGES FOR CLEAR CHANNEL)

Pink appearing on the US ABC TV talk show *The View* before performing 'Blow Me (One Last Kiss)'.
(LOU ROCCO/ABC VIA GETTY IMAGES)

Pink onstage during the 2012 MTV Video Music Awards at the Staples Center, Los Angeles, September 6, 2012.
(JEFF KRAVITZ/FILMMAGIC)

Pink in gymnast mode during the 2012 MTV Video Music Awards, performing '(Blow Me) One Last Kiss'.
(JEFF KRAVITZ/FILMMAGIC)

Pink onstage at the US Airways Center, Phoenix, Arizona, during the Truth About Love tour, February 13, 2013.
(KEVIN MAZUR/WIREIMAGE)

Trapeze-y does it: Pink at the Manchester Academy on April 14, 2013. (SHIRLAINE FORREST/WIREIMAGE)

With its success, Pink reconciled herself to the idea of a document of her finest work to date. "Record companies can put out compilations without your permission," she said, but she decided that, after seeing the finished product, she felt "less skeptical" about it; she even "started to feel a little proud."

Pink had every reason to feel proud of her occasional forays into the world of cinema. During the first couple of years of the new decade, following bit parts in 2002's *Rollerball* and 2003's *Charlie's Angels: Full Throttle*, and a larger role in 2007 horror flick *Catacombs*, she finally joined the ranks of the A-list (alongside the likes of Elijah Wood and Robin Williams) when she provided the voice for the character of Gloria in *Happy Feet Two*, which premiered in November 2011 in the US (she also sang the theme song, 'Bridge Of Light'). And she had her first leading role in a movie when she starred alongside Gwyneth Paltrow and Mark Ruffalo in *Thanks For Sharing*. A comedy-drama – increasingly widely known as a "dramedy" – about sex addiction that premiered at the Toronto International Film Festival in September 2012, it saw Pink playing the part of Dede, a 30-year-old tattooed tough-girl who finds it difficult relating to men outside of the bedroom, hence her recourse to sexual therapy and the support group that provides the focus for much of the story. The singer acquitted herself well, according to the critics, many remarking that she acted better than Paltrow.

"Pink proves a capable actor and a relaxed, enormously likable screen presence," wrote the *Hollywood Reporter* while *Indiewire* concluded that she was "a truly pleasant surprise in her first major screen outing (not counting animated gigs)."

If 2011 was a relatively slow year for Pink, musically at least, with just 'Bridge Of Light' seeing a single release, which only became a moderate hit in Australia and parts of Europe, then 2012 saw her back to something approaching full throttle. In

February she announced on Twitter that she was amassing songs for her next studio album, her sixth, and that it would be released in September.

Ahead of that there was a single, which suggested that the usual pop star burnout and loss of inspiration would not be problems for Pink, now enjoying her third decade as a performer. Premiered on her official website in July, 'Blow Me (One Last Kiss)' had the impish energy and cheeky wit of a debut single by a brand new artist with plenty to prove. From its double-entendre title onwards, this was a break-up song full of attitude but with the immediacy of her most successful work. 'Blow Me (One Last Kiss)' was an object lesson in how to construct the perfect radio hit. It came as no surprise, then, to learn that it had been co-written with Greg Kurstin, hitmaker for Britney Spears and Lily Allen, Kelly Clarkson, Ke$ha and Kylie Minogue. Here was someone with an innate understanding of the dynamics of pop song construction and it showed throughout the four minutes and 16 seconds of 'Blow Me (One Last Kiss)', which was like sixties girl group pop put through a grunge-lite filter. As Pink sang the chorus, "I've had a shit, you've had a shit day, we've had a shit day", followed by the "la-la-la" refrain, it was like some dream team-up between Courtney Love and the Shangri-Las.

"I think you're going to like it, because I really like it, and I like it enough for all of us," Pink said at the time while Kurstin revealed that they had problems coming up with a name for the track. "She kept coming back to, 'Let's throw in the towel'," he said, alluding to Pink's feeling that they should perhaps scrap it, before it occurred that that was actually the gist of the song. "It was one of those things where we had to say, 'Is that line really the song?'" Kurstin recalled. "So then I came back with 'Blow me… one last kiss' and we got really excited. Most of the time with

Pink she's so strong writing lyrics I don't really interfere. I let her do her thing. That could've been the only time I did that."

Pink's 29th single was met with enthusiastic reviews. *Billboard* called it "an empowering breakup anthem in the vein of 'So What'" and described Pink as a "veteran pop star" whose performance on the single was as "feisty, energetic and vengeful as ever". Others noted Pink's "signature sass" and the song's undeniably "poppy hook".

The critical acclaim for 'Blow Me (One Last Kiss)' was matched by its commercial performance. Propelled by a Dave Meyers-helmed black and white (with tinges of red) video that saw Pink, in a pastiche of or homage to sixties French cinema, whisked from pillar to post by various handsome men, ending with the star leaving a wedding scene on a flying bike, it reached number one in Australia, Hungary and Scotland and the top three in the UK, Brazil, Japan and Croatia. In the States it peaked at number five and sold a million copies, confirming Pink's staying power as, along with Rihanna and Beyoncé, the most prolific female hitmaker in the US since the new century was ushered in. It also became Pink's 10th consecutive German number one, the most ever achieved by an artist there.

In September, Pink performed a cleaned-up version of the single at the 2012 MTV Video Music Awards, on *The Ellen DeGeneres Show* and on British TV's *Alan Carr: Chatty Man* comedy show, and performed the uncensored version on *The Daily Show* with Jon Stewart.

That same month saw the release, on RCA Records, of Pink's sixth album, *The Truth About Love*. With featured guests including Eminem, Lily Allen (referred to in the credits by her married name of Lily Rose Cooper) and Nate Ruess of fast-rising US band Fun (who, with their worldwide smash, 'We Are Young' featuring Janelle Monáe, boasted one of 2012's radio staples), it was a no-holds-barred attempt by Pink to retain her crown as America's premier punk-pop princess.

The sleeve, depicting our heroine dressed in stockings, suspenders and red stilettos, showed she was in no mood for compromise, and suggested that this would not be her mature coming-of-age album. No, this was quintessential Pink, a feeling confirmed by opening track 'Are We All We Are', with its faux crowd cheers at the start announcing the star in no uncertain terms. The first of many ear-worms and catchy chant-worthy anthems, 'Are We All We Are' was pop-grunge, like Nirvana if they'd been fronted by a feisty girl from Pennsylvania. With its forceful, driving riff and cute-girl repetition of the title, it found Pink in empowering mode, declaring that she'd "had it up to here" and urging her audience to "take the power back". 'Blow Me (One Last Kiss)' hinted at one problem presented by *The Truth About Love*: how to decide which songs to release as singles, so spoilt for choice was Pink's record company. Track three, 'Try', a collaboration with Michael James Ryan Busbee and Ben West – who between them had penned hits for Katy Perry, Christina Aguilera, Lady Antebellum and Flo Rida – was actually the song chosen to be the second single from *The Truth About Love* in October 2012. With its descending piano motif, grinding guitars and pounding bass, it was far slower and moodier than its predecessor, with the quiet-loud dynamic of a Nirvana classic, making it sound like a sort of latterday, pop-wise version of Kurt Cobain's 'Come As You Are'. Even the lyrics were Cobain-style angst-lite about getting "burned", although because this was aimed at the charts the sense of despondency and ennui in the face of life/love's travails was tempered by a positive message ("You've got to get up and try").

Listened to with the benefit of hindsight, *The Truth About Love* can seem like Pink's Greatest Hits Volume 2, because the fourth track on the album became the third one lifted off the record for single release the following February. 'Just Give Me A Reason' was a dark rock ballad that presented Pink at the start as "your willing victim". The song grew louder and more rhythmic as fun's Nate Ruess, sounding like a toned-down Freddie Mercury, joined in the fun. "It's been written in the scars on our hearts/We're not broken just bent/And we can learn to love again," went the chorus, a strange rallying cry, perhaps, but somehow it worked on this song for the downtrodden in love, the bloody but unbowed. The next track, 'True Love', was another single, albeit only in Hungary (where it reached number 36 in January 2013). Here, Pink was in no more of a conciliatory mood, admonishing the subject of her scorn with the line, "Sometimes I hate every single stupid word you say" and referring to him as "an asshole" while issuing the warning that he (or she) might just drive her to physical violence. But there was a twist, because it was the fact that she felt so strongly about him (or her) that convinced her this must be the titular feeling, hence the perky nature of the song. With Lily Allen providing cute cooing backing vocals and a bouncy middle-eight, this was another triumph, a showcase for the US and UK's twin titans of grrrl power and female 'tood.

'How Come You're Not Here' was an uptempo rocker that added to the vengeful atmosphere and offered further evidence that *The Truth About Love* was an opportunity for Pink to explore her emotions with regard to her tempestuous relationship with her husband, Carey Hart. One of many Pink-Kurstin numbers on the album, 'How Come You're Not Here' was rock with a pop sheen that found Pink channelling her inner Suzi Quatro and Joan Jett, with a knock-out chorus that was almost glam rocky in its bubblegum catchiness. 'Slut Like You' was a Pink co-write with Max Martin and Shellback that, like 'How

Come...', could easily have been a huge hit single, even given the title and lyrics. "I'm not a slut," declared Pink at the start, with a giggle, "I just love love." An indecently infectious pop-punk stomper to rival Blur's 'Song 2', with a similar "wooh-ooh" refrain and some deft couplets ("You think you call the shots – I just bought you some"), 'Slut Like You' again showed Pink had lost none of her fizz or R-rated sparkle.

The title track was another of the album's roughed-up girl group revisits and attempts to subvert love tropes, presenting the raw, unvarnished truth about love while allying it to a melody and rhythm as pretty and perky as any ditzy sixties pop hit you care to mention, handclaps, harmonies and all. 'Beam Me Up' was a gritty, heartfelt ballad written by Billy Mann. 'Walk Of Shame' was a Pink/Kurstin gem about the morning after the night before with explicit lyrics and musical gusto to match the lyrical bravado. 'Here Comes The Weekend' featured Eminem, returning the favour for Pink's cameo on his album. 'Where Did The Beat Go?' featured a descending melody and mournful chord sequence and recalled the sort of quirkily rhythmic R&B Pink began her career with. 'The Great Escape', a country-rock ballad co-penned by Dan Wilson of indie rockers Semisonic, was the closing track of the official album.

There were several extra tracks made available for different versions of the album in various territories. 'My Signature Move' was staccato piano-based pop-rock, anthemic and rous-ing, that sounded like Bruce Springsteen meeting David Bowie in the late-seventies. 'Is This Thing On?' was a lovely, melodramatic number and a sure sign of the record company's confidence in the material, that this should be consigned to extra-material status. 'Run' was a distinctive ballad that you easily imagine being a stadium singalong for lighters-wielding fans. Finally, there was 'Good Old Days', a sprightly, uplifting affair that belied the reflective, melancholy nature of the lyrics.

If anything, these were Pink's good old days. The album debuted at number one in Australia, Austria, Canada, Germany, New Zealand, Sweden and Switzerland. It became Australia's biggest-selling album of the year, her third album to achieve that feat there. Most crucially, *The Truth About Love* entered the US charts at number one, her first album to do so, and sold nearly 300,000 copies in America in its first week.

"I've never been this pleasantly received before," said a clearly delighted Pink. "It's my first number one album anywhere except Australia." She added that "this is the dream I had when I was four, and now I've done it. I no longer feel like the underdog with a point to prove."

The album earned some of the best reviews of Pink's career. *The Guardian* decided she was "easily the most idiosyncratic of the current cohort of high-gloss American pop singers – the only one bold enough to write songs that give free rein to her ugly, brattish side." The newspaper added: "She funnels her thoughts into some of the most pungent songs in pop. She also has the nous to convert raw emotion into pop-punk earworms." *Entertainment Weekly* called it a "lyrical masterpiece" and hailed Pink's contributions as "unfalteringly vibrant, loaded with righteous anger, irreverence, and a clear eye for the darker side." *Billboard* dubbed the album "a peerlessly witty, endlessly melodic tour de force."

There were some nay-sayers. *Spin* described it as "pop karaoke" while *Rolling Stone* found Pink devolving "into self-parody" and the *Chicago Tribune* complained about the "formula production and hack songwriting". Nevertheless, *The Truth About Love* became Pink's second consecutive album to receive a Grammy Award nomination for Best Pop Vocal

Album (even though, in February 2013, it eventually lost out to Kelly Clarkson's *Stronger*) and by the end of 2012 it had sold nearly two million copies worldwide.

To further promote the album, Pink embarked on her Truth About Love tour in February 2013. The *Hollywood Reporter* noted that, with Lady Gaga out of action with a damaged hip, "Pink's acrobatic-heavy *Truth About Love* tour proves to be pop's biggest spectacle". Pink, of course, had used acrobatics on her 2009 Funhouse tour, but this latest foray saw her perfect her routines and take them to the next level, with the star – all dolled up in a gold bodysuit and strapped into a harness – suspended high above the stage by three muscular male dancers, singing 'Raise Your Glass' as she was slingshotted back into the air with a bungee-like contraption. And that was just the introduction! Elsewhere, there were video screens (including one giant heart-shaped one), staircases and light posts, a crew of dancers, a five-piece band, a pair of backing singers, various costume changes and an MC. If Pink was under siege from the newer female artists, she was hardly going to cede any pop ground without a fight.

The second single released from *The Truth About Love* was 'Try', which went Top 10 in 14 countries, including number nine in the US, throughout autumn and winter 2012. The making of the accompanying video was, Pink stated, "The most fun I've ever had in my entire career. I never wanted it to end. It's my favourite video ever." More lyrical than the star's usual comical fare, the promo has been viewed upwards of 56 million times on Pink's official Vevo channel on YouTube.

RCA issued a third single from *The Truth About Love* in early 2013. 'Just Give Me A Reason' was accompanied by a video featuring not just guest vocalist Nate Ruess but Carey Hart, her husband. Despite reports that they had divorced some time in the noughties, she and the motocross champion were not just still married, they were happier than ever, and with a baby daughter, Willow, to add to the picture of domestic bliss. *The Truth About Love* may have been Pink-style angry business as usual, but the fact was, she had seemingly exorcised a lot of the demons that had damaged the relationship over the years, and she had managed to isolate all her negative emotions, keeping them in the realm of her art.

Indeed, in December 2012, when she was interviewed by Britain's *Daily Telegraph*, the journalist worried that a content, domesticated Pink might mean the singer would lose all the impetus for her art. Did this, asked Helena De Bertodano, mean the end of Pink as we know her?

"No way," she replied. "When you have a dark side nothing is ever as good as it seems."

She continued: "I guess people look at me and say, 'You're happy; what could you possibly have to add?' I'm married, my life is more real than ever. I'm still engaged in the world, I'm still a career mom, I still have a relationship I'm trying to keep."

True enough. As De Bertodano pointed out, she and Hart's relationship had hardly been plain sailing. After all, they met in 2001 and married in 2006, then split up in 2008, only to reconcile in 2009, ahead of the birth of their daughter in 2011. In addition, she had the memory of her parents' own turbulent relationship from which to draw for her music. She sang about their arguments on her early track 'Family Portrait' ("Daddy, please stop yelling, I can't stand the sound/Make Mama stop crying, 'cause I need you around"). As she told the *Telegraph*: "That was my life. I was a daddy's girl and I was devastated when he left because my mom and I never really got along. But it was also, 'God, what a relief.' You spend the first nine years of your life afraid of what's going to happen in your house and then you just have quiet. I flinch now when people fight. I can't handle it."

As to whether she fought with her husband, she laughed and answered honestly: "I do, and passionately. But I don't have to listen to it as I'm yelling louder than he is. We used to fight a lot more, especially when we were drinking. He's Italian-Irish and so stubborn. I'm, like, 'Have some more Jameson [whiskey]. You're on the couch again.'"

In 2012, VH1 placed Pink at number 10 on its list of the 100 Greatest Women in Music. Around the same time, James Montgomery of MTV described her as "a fabulously fearless pop artist" who can "out-sing almost anyone out there. She can out-crazy Gaga or Lily. She's the total pop-star package, everything you'd want in a singer/entertainer/icon." Even Adele, arguably the most popular singer/entertainer/icon on the planet during 2011-12, got in on the act, citing Pink's performance at Brixton Academy in London circa the *Missundaztood* album, as one of the "defining moments" of her young life.

"I was 13 or 14," she recalled, "and I had never heard, being in the room, someone sing like that live. I remember sort of feeling like I was in a wind tunnel, her voice just hitting me. It was incredible."

After over a decade in the public eye, Pink was still making converts.

"My husband is, like, 'Hey, it only took you nine years to get people to like you,'" she joked to the reporter from *The Daily Telegraph*. "I'm like, 'It took me nine years to like you, too…'"

Finally, asked to define her appeal, pop's eternal outsider thought for a moment before replying.

"I don't live in the Hollywood bubble," she decided. "I never have and I never will. I wasn't invited to that party." She paused for comic effect. "And if I was, I'd probably arrive late and be dressed inappropriately."

Acknowledgements

Even though this is an unauthorised book, nevertheless there are several people at Pink's record company, particularly Chris Latham and Fun Cheung, who helped make it possible and proved invaluable when it came to the business of granting access to Sony/BMG's pile of press cuttings and trove of obscure Australian import Pink CDs. Thanks must also go to the author's children – Ben, Ethan and Talia – who were forced to listen to nothing but Pink for most of the first half of 2009 when really they were dying to return to their normal diet of Throbbing Gristle and Destiny's Child. Finally, as ever, a special mention to Chris Charlesworth of Omnibus Press, whose patience was sorely tried despite my treating deadlines with the sort of cavalier regard that Pink treats her men. Probably.

Acknowledgements

Discography

CAN'T TAKE ME HOME (2000)
Split Personality (Terence 'Tramp Baby' Abney, Babyface,
A. Moore), Hell Wit Ya (Kevin 'She'kspere' Briggs,
Kandi Burruss, D. Green, Moore), Most Girls (Babyface,
D. Thomas), There You Go (Briggs, Burruss, Moore),
You Make Me Sick (B. Dimilo, Anthony President,
M. Tabb), Let Me Let You Know (N. Creque, S. Hall,
C. Stewart, R. Thicke), Love Is Such A Crazy Thing
(J. Boyd, D. Jones, M. Keith, L. Maxwell, Q. Parker,
M. Scandrick, C. Sills), Private Show (K. Karlin, A. Martin,
I. Matias, C. Schack, L. Schack), Can't Take Me Home
(Steve "Rhythm" Clarke, Moore), Stop Falling (W. Baker,
Moore, P. Woodruff), Do What U Do (J. Hollins, E. Lewis,
K. Prather, M. Sinclair), Hiccup (D. Avant, Clarke, Moore),
Is It Love (Clarke, Moore, A. Phillips)

M!SSUNDAZTOOD (2001)

M!ssundaztood (Linda Perry, Pink), Don't Let Me Get Me (Dallas Austin, Pink), Just Like A Pill (Austin, Pink), Get The Party Started (Perry), Respect (Perry, Pink) featuring Scratch, 18 Wheeler (Austin, Pink), Family Portrait (Pink, Scott Storch), Misery (Richie Supa) featuring Steven Tyler, Dear Diary (Perry, Pink), Eventually (Perry, Pink), Lonely Girl (Perry) featuring Linda Perry, Numb (Austin, Pink), Gone To California (Perry, Pink), My Vietnam (Perry, Pink)

TRY THIS (2003)

Trouble (Tim Armstrong, Pink), God Is A DJ (Billy Mann, Jonathan Davis, Pink), Last To Know (Armstrong, Pink), Tonight's The Night (Armstrong, Pink) featuring Peaches, Oh My God (Armstrong, Merrill Nisker, Pink), Catch Me While I'm Sleeping (Linda Perry, Pink), Waiting For Love (Paul Ill, Brian MacLeod, Perry, Pink, Eric Schermerhorn), Save My Life (Armstrong, Pink), Try Too Hard (Perry, Pink), Humble Neighborhoods (Armstrong, Pink), Walk Away (Armstrong, Pink), Unwind (Armstrong, Pink), Feel Good Time (William Orbit, Beck Hansen, Jay Ferguson), Love Song (Damon Elliott, Pink)

I'M NOT DEAD (2006)

Stupid Girls (Pink, Billy Mann, Robin Mortensen Lynch), Who Knew (Pink, Max Martin, Lukasz Gottwald), Long Way To Happy (Pink, Butch Walker), Nobody Knows (Mann, Pink), Dear Mr. President (Pink, Mann) featuring Indigo Girls, I'm Not Dead (Pink, Mann), Cuz I Can (Pink, Martin, Gottwald), Leave Me Alone (I'm Lonely) (Pink, Walker), U + Ur Hand (Pink, Martin, Gottwald, Rami), Runaway (Pink, Mann), The One That Got Away

(Pink, Mann), I Got Money Now (Pink, Mike Elizondo),
Conversations With My 13 Year Old Self (Pink, Mann),
I Have Seen The Rain (Pink, Mann, Christopher Rojas),
Heartbreaker (Pink, William Wells, Kara DioGuardi)
featuring James T. Moore, Fingers (Pink, Greg Kurstin,
Cathy Dennis)

FUNHOUSE (2008)
So What (Pink, Max Martin, Shellback), Sober (Pink,
Nathaniel Hills, Kara DioGuardi, Marcella Araica), I Don't
Believe You (Pink, Martin), One Foot Wrong (Pink, Francis
White), Please Don't Leave Me (Pink, Martin), Bad
Influence (Pink, Billy Mann, Butch Walker, MachoPsycho),
Funhouse (Pink, Tony Kanal, Jimmy Harry), Crystal Ball
(Pink, Mann), Mean (Pink, Walker), It's All Your Fault
(Pink, Martin, Shellback), Ave Mary A (Pink, Mann, Pete
Wallace), Glitter In The Air (Pink, Mann), This Is How It
Goes Down (Pink, Mann), Could've Had Everything
(Pink, Eg White), Why Did I Ever Like You (Pink, Greg
Wells), Boring (Pink, Martin, Shellback)

GREATEST HITS ... SO FAR (2010)
Get The Party Started, There You Go, Don't Let Me Get Me,
Just Like A Pill, Family Portrait, Trouble, Stupid Girls, Who
Knew, U + Ur Hand, Dear Mr President, So What, Sober,
Please Don't Leave Me, Glitter In The Air, Raise Your Glass,
F★★★kin' Perfect (Pink, Max Martin, Shellback)

THE TRUTH ABOUT LOVE (2012)
Are We All We Are (Pink, Butch Walker, John Hill, Emile
Haynie), Blow Me (One Last Kiss) (Pink, Greg Kurstin,
busbee, Ben West), Just Give Me A Reason (Pink, Jeff

Bhasker, Nate Ruess), True Love (Pink, Kurstin, Cooper),
How Come You're Not Here (Pink, Kurstin), Slut Like You
(Pink, Max Martin, Shellback), The Truth About Love (Pink,
Billy Mann, David Schuler), Beam Me Up (Pink, Mann),
Walk Of Shame (Pink, Kurstin), Here Comes The Weekend
(Pink, Khalil Abdul Rahman, Pranam Injeti, Liz Rodrigues,
Marshall Mathers), Where Did The Beat Go? (Pink, Mann,
Jon Keep, Steve Daly), The Great Escape (Pink, Dan Wilson)